Rethinking matching
in adoptions from care

Rethinking matching in adoptions from care
A conceptual and research review

David Quinton

Published by British Association
for Adoption & Fostering
(BAAF)
Saffron House
3rd Floor, 6–10 Kirby Street
London EC1N 8TS
www.baaf.org.uk

Charity registration 275689 (England and Wales)
and SC039337 (Scotland)

© David Quinton, 2012

British Library Cataloguing in Publication Data
A catalogue record for this book is available
from the British Library

ISBN 978 1 907585 23 4

Editorial project management by Jo Francis, BAAF Publications
Designed by Helen Joubert Associates
Typeset by Avon DataSet Ltd, Bidford on Avon
Printed in Great Britain by TJ International
Trade distribution by Turnaround Publisher Services,
Unit 3, Olympia Trading Estate, Coburg Road,
London N22 6TZ

BAAF is the leading UK-wide membership
organisation for all those concerned with
adoption, fostering and child care issues.

Contents

Acknowledgements

Matching children and adopters is a very complex task and my thinking on the topic has been guided, challenged and affected by many people. First, it is necessary to thank the then Department for Children, Schools and Families (DCSF) for funding the Adoption Research Initiative, with which this review is associated and especially to thank Caroline Thomas, the Co-ordinator of the Initiative, for unfailing support and encouragement.

Academic and practice colleagues have discussed the issues around matching with me over the years, all of whom I would like to acknowledge. First, Julie Selwyn, Director of the Hadley Centre for Adoption and Foster Care Studies at the University of Bristol and all those involved in the related study of *Pathways to Permanence for Black, Asian and Mixed Ethnicity Children*: Dinithi Wijedasa, Perlita Harris, Shameem Nawaz and Marsha Wood. Second, practice colleagues who gave their time and expertise in discussions on how matching was done, especially Dr Corinne Rees from the Tyndall's Park Children's Centre; Peter Wrighton and Julie Cook from BAAF South West England; Kate O'Brien, Adoption Planning Manager with Bristol City Council; and from the BAAF Head Office, John Simmonds, Jenny Cousins and Louise Hocking; and Andy Stott, Adoption Register Manager.

Finally, I would like to include, from a long research history, colleagues by whom I have been greatly stimulated and encouraged over the years, especially Alan Rushton and Cherilyn Dance and, of course, Karen John for ongoing discussions at home.

Despite all this input, the conclusions expressed in this review are entirely my own. I hope that all of those named above will agree with most of them, but I do not expect anyone to agree with all. The review should not be taken necessarily to reflect the views of the Department for Education.

Note about the author

David Quinton is Emeritus Professor of Psychosocial Development in the School for Policy Studies at the University of Bristol, and founder of the Hadley Centre for Adoption and Foster Care Studies. He read English and Social Anthropology at the University of Cambridge and, following a year as a Commonwealth Scholar in Nigeria at the University of Ibadan, he worked for 30 years in the Department of Child and Adolescent Psychiatry and the MRC Child Psychiatry Unit at the Institute of Psychiatry in London on longitudinal studies on the long-term effects of childhood experiences on psychosocial functioning. He also worked on the Maudsley Adoption Studies there. He moved to the University of Bristol in 1994 as part of the expansion of the School for Policy Studies. He co-ordinated the Department of Health's research initiative, 'Supporting Parents', and set up the Hadley Centre as a way of bringing research and practice closer together. Since retirement, he has continued to work with the Centre, but has also worked on the developmental process at work in the plants in the garden and in his grandchildren.

Preface

It is difficult to imagine a more life-changing act than placing a child with adopters. The consequences of that decision for the child, the adopters and the birth parents could be compared to heart transplants in the way that it is intended to transform a life. But that maybe underestimates the complexity, the benefits and the risks of that matching decision. It also doesn't quite capture the profound working out of feelings of love, loss and change that are so much a part of adoption. There is also one more difference: heart, or indeed any form of transplant surgery, has a substantial knowledge and evidence base to it – which organs can be transplanted in what context to ensure the survival of the recipient. There is also a substantial skill base in the teams of people who perform such surgical procedures.

One would assume that matching children with adopters, given the enormity of what it is intended to do, would be performed with similar degrees of knowledge, evidence and skill. And that is the task that David Quinton has set himself. What do we know about these whole body transplants – physical, social and emotional – that ensures that they transform the lives of the child and the adopters in the way that is intended and needed? It couldn't be a more important question to ask and it couldn't have been a more difficult question to find an answer to.

The issues, evidence and answers that David Quinton presents here are in some ways anticipated, in some ways a surprise, and in some ways troubling. Matching in adoption can't really be compared to organ transplants – the knowledge base is poor, particularly the characteristics of children that match with the identified characteristics of adopters. The skill base is not well articulated in ensuring that the match is performed well. And it is nothing like as well resourced as surgery is. We need to know more and we need to draw on a skill base that is far more reliable, available and better resourced than it currently is.

But despite these serious gaps that are fully and with great insight explored here, there is still a sense that, overall, adoption works well. So despite working in something of a vacuum when compared to other professions, adoption professionals manage to find their way into doing a good enough job given what we know about the good outcomes in adoption. Lives are indeed transformed for the good in the greater majority of cases. But for some adoptions there are too many examples of continuing and serious struggles and for some, disruption.

As Quinton so clearly demonstrates, the evidence base for explaining difficulties and disruptions is still poor. In retrospect, it is often possible to identify what wasn't really addressed in matching when things do go wrong – the thoroughness in assessing and understanding the child's needs or the needs of the adopters or the degree of fit between them. But predicting these issues is, as Quinton says, more art than science, although science has its part to play. While reinforcing the need for there to be further development of an evidence-based framework, it seems particularly important to acknowledge that matching as a predictive science is still very much in its infancy. It works and works well enough through the application of professional experience and knowledge with a high loading of intuition. Acknowledging what is known is clearly critical and that is why this text needs to become well known and thoroughly thumbed through.

But the systems and processes that manage the matching process must openly acknowledge the presence of imperfection. Professional practice often does not easily lend itself to openness about what isn't known or can't be predicted, especially when the consequences are so profound. But openness in relation to matching should be a route into acknowledging that staying in touch, continuing to be engaged, finding ways of sorting problems out and providing support to adoptive families are what balances the risk inherent in this, the most profound of professional decisions.

John Simmonds
Director of Policy, Research and Development, BAAF

Executive summary

Purpose

This review is about the matching of children to families in adoption, the intentions behind this process, the beliefs and principles on which this is based, and the evidence on its effectiveness. It is a review of *concepts and research evidence* in relation to matching. It is not a comprehensive review of the literature on adoption and permanent placements or of opinions or advice on practice where these are currently un-researched. Nor is it a review of unpublished accounts of practice, nor a survey of current practice approaches. This review is restricted to a discussion of the implications of the conceptual framework surrounding matching and to a summary of the ways in which research can help in taking the matching enterprise forward.

At the time this review was completed and since, there has been a period of rapid policy development, which has not yet been completed and which has not, therefore, been fully reflected in official documents or recommended practice advice. The author has done his best to understand the policy context at the time that the review was written. Any errors are entirely due to his failure to achieve sufficient understanding. Readers are advised to check the current position. A good source is the BAAF website's tracking of policy and research news and updates, e.g. www.baaf.org.uk/res/links#advice/ or www. baaf.org.uk/res/law.

Background

Matching children's needs and adoptive parents' capacities is seen as key to increasing the stability of adoptive placements and of improving outcomes. This has been written into a number of practice guidelines since the Children Act 1989. In addition, the matching process is also required by law to '. . . give due consideration to the child's religious persuasion, racial origin and cultural and linguistic background'

(Adoption and Children Act, 2002, s.1(5)) although attempts to match on these characteristics have to be balanced against the negative effects of delay. *This requirement contrasts with policy in the US where taking ethnicity into account when matching is unlawful.*

These objectives are based both on beliefs that research evidence supports the idea of matching *and* on beliefs about what is right and proper in decisions about the best placement of children who need alternative families. These views are most clearly apparent in instances where matching on ethnicity and culture is an issue.

Prior to the Children Act 1989, the matching of children and adoptive parents was primarily concerned with preserving religious affiliations or finding children who looked like the members of the families they entered. Placement itself was seen as sufficient to deal with the welfare issue. The Children Act extended the idea of the Welfare Principle and the requirement to match children with specific needs with parents who could meet these needs, and to provide services to help the children and the adopters in this. This is now the guiding principle for policy and practice.

However, given the emphasis now placed on the matching process, the word "matching" occurs only infrequently in official documents. These documents seldom give even broad definitions of key terms such as: "needs", "capacities", "racial origin" or "cultural background". The assessment of needs, capacities and appropriate service responses is set out in the Assessment Framework and related documents, together with a methodology for doing this through systematic record keeping. This approach is currently under review because of reactions to the "tick-box" culture. Practitioners are often left to their own experience, presumptions and practice pressures in making decisions.

Assessing children's needs and parental capacities

It seems obvious to try to link needs and capacities when considering the permanent placement of children with "substitute" parents. However, what should be included under either of these headings is unclear, and there has been no published discussion on how fine the matching should be.

Meeting children's needs

The idea of "meeting needs" is central to current legislation and practice guidance on adoption, the primacy of the welfare principle and the importance of a "secure environment", for which "permanence" is a prerequisite, in providing for the child's welfare. A further legal requirement is that due consideration is given to the child's religious persuasion, ethnic origin and cultural and linguistic background. Beyond these general requirements, which effectively set a hierarchy in matching decisions, the setting out of what "needs" are to be taken into account is left to practice guidance, which usually follows the seven areas of child development set out in the *Assessment Framework* (DH, DfES and Home Office, 2000). Unfortunately, there are no data that shed any light on how well these areas of difficulty are or can be assessed prior to placement, especially in the early years of life, and following a pattern of disturbed parenting and parenting contexts.

There is also a lack of good information on how the assessment of children's needs is carried out and on whether these assessments are adequate and reliable. The terminology is also rather grand, for example, it is not clear how we might know that needs have been met. In practice – and not unreasonably – what is more often meant is: 'do the best we can to help this child and the adopters'.

The assessment of the key child drivers of placement success or instability – behavioural problems, over-activity and restlessness, and difficulties in making relationships ("attachment" in a broad sense) – is left to the experience and "practice wisdom" of those making the assessments, using the Child Permanence Report, and their judgement on when to call for expert opinion. Advice on assessing these is lacking, as indeed are good guidelines on what might be taken into account.

Child assessments ought to be based on knowledge of child development, training in systematic assessments, and an ability to put the child's psychosocial development in context. At the time this report was written, systematic assessments of emotional and behavioural development and attachment were rare, so that judgements relied on the experience and knowledge of the assessor, sometimes backed up by expert opinions. Implementing systems to provide systematic assessments, such as the Integrated Children's System (Department of Health, 2002a), has been difficult. At present, it is not known how common it is for those undertaking child assessments to have such expertise but, anecdotally, the quality of assessments is reported as very variable. This is apparent in research studies using case notes.

Because the assessment of developmental needs is difficult with young children, judgements based on the possible consequences of prior experiences necessarily come into play. For this reason, assessment is bound to be a somewhat speculative procedure in the first instance, beyond the identification of obviously serious difficulties.

For this reason alone, matching must be seen as an ongoing process in which both long-term difficulties and emerging problems can be identified quickly and handled as well as is possible. This points to the importance of the willingness of adopters to work with the agency on a continuing basis and the capacity of the agency to offer responsive and expert advice and assistance.

Assessing parents' capacities

Positive parenting capacities identified by research for all children include: warmth, positive regard, boundary setting, and social and experiential facilitation. In addition, adoptive parents need some special capacities: commitment to children who are not birth children; a flexible and relaxed approach to parenting; realistic expectations; the ability to distance themselves from the child's behaviour, including tolerance of a lack of closeness; sensitivity to attachments to adults outside the family; and a willingness to work with the agency.

Assessment of parenting is much more developed than the assessment of children's needs, at least as far as resource guides and training materials are concerned. But the quality of these assessments, including the use of standardised measures, depends on training, supervision and support. Lack of adequate training can lead to the superficial take-up of new knowledge, for example, on "attachment" and "resilience". Many workers are reported to feel starved of training on assessment.

Research suggests that the assessment of adopters can work well in screening out obviously unsuitable applicants and picking those who have the general capacities to provide secure placements for children. New approaches such as "adopter-led" matching are trying, with some success, to bring the otherwise unknowable element of "fit" or "click" into play, although well-evaluated accounts of these are lacking.

Matching on ethnicity

An argument is made in support of the term "ethnicity" instead of "race" in discussions of child welfare. The predominant view amongst geneticists and sociologists is that the term "race" is a social construction that is not biologically meaningful. Rather, the use of the term reflects relationships of power, domination and oppression, through which a group can be treated differentially in economic and social ways because of 'observed or imagined bodily features pre-sumed to be evidence of an ancestral link to a certain geographic region' (Haslanger, 2008). The continued use of the term in social policy and political discussions seems appropriate *only* when it refers to abuses of power and to actions deriving from mistaken beliefs about essential differences. That is, when it refers to "racism".

Taking ethnicity into account in matching is given priority in the UK context but is unlawful in the United States. To match on ethnicity can be problematic because of over-inclusive definitions (e.g. the label "Asian"), and also because the majority of minority ethnic children for whom adoptive placements are sought – approximately three-quarters – are of mixed heritage, usually of white mothers and minority ethnic fathers.

The issue of matching on ethnicity is complicated because it involves not only the developmental outcomes of the children, but also the rights and beliefs of cultural groups and birth parents on whom the children "belong to". Satisfying these cultural needs does not depend on evidence of measurable effects on psychosocial development, providing that the match does not go against the Welfare Principle. However, these arguments commonly draw on research into psychosocial outcomes for support.

Ethnic matching is encouraged because it is believed to lead to improved psychosocial outcomes, a more secure "racial" identity and greater capacity to cope with racism. The evidence for these arguments is not strong. Disruption rates for matched and not-matched children are much the same and there are few differences in most psychosocial outcomes or self-esteem, although there are some differences on identification with being black, with trans-ethnically placed children often less attached to their ethnic group or its heritage. Research evidence is also equivocal with regard to the enhanced preparedness to cope with racism, which same-ethnicity placements are strongly believed to provide, although it does suggest that the sensitivity of non-matched adopters to problems with racism is an important element.

A counter-argument is that these studies omit important aspects of outcome or are not sensitive enough, an argument that has some force. On the other hand, the debate gives insufficient attention to young people's own agency in constructing their identities. There can also be an assumption about what the children's identity *ought* to be, even when a child seems content with his or her own self-image and identification.

Key conclusions

- There is virtually no research on the extent to which children's needs are matched with the capacities of adoptive parents to meet them. For this reason, we do not know to what extent attention to matching makes a difference to outcomes or not.
- The most useful research findings come from studies on the predictors of adoption disruption, but few studies consider child and adopter predictors at the same time. A few prospective studies have shown that some parenting styles are better at containing children with particular needs, but these studies were not set up as studies of matching; that is, whether the matching process itself made these advantageous matches.
- The assessment of children's needs in the matching process is conceptually and practically under-developed. Lists of needs in practice advice include a great variety of behaviours and circumstances, but few of these are well defined. At present, the

assessment of needs is neither systematic nor detailed enough to facilitate the matching of needs and capacities.

- The characteristics of children that predict adoption disruption include: age at placement; previous disruptions; maltreatment or rejection by birth parents; and attachment to or disturbed contact with the birth family. These factors probably have their impact through conduct difficulties, overactivity and restlessness (ADHD), and a failure to attach to the adoptive family.
- The assessment of parenting capacities is more developed. The parental characteristics related to stability include: commitment; a flexible and relaxed approach to parenting; realistic expectations; the ability to distance themselves from the child's behaviour; a willingness to work with the agency; and an understanding that information about the child is related to success.
- Evaluating matches made within or across ethnicities is problematic, firstly because the majority of minority ethnic children adopted from care in the UK are of mixed white/minority ethnic parentage; and secondly because ethnic matching involves issues of rights as well as psychosocial outcomes.
- A strong argument is made for reconceptualising matching as an ongoing process in which agency actions and support are seen as part of the ecology of parenting, not simply something that takes place prior to placement or is "put in" when difficulties arise. This is necessarily the case because "needs" can only be truly assessed once a placement is under way and because adopters themselves have needs as well as capacities. Adopters and agencies need to work together to discover the children's needs as these become apparent and to tailor services to support the children and the adopters.

Implications

There are a number of implications from this review.

- The concepts and definitions used in policy and practice documents on matching need more consideration and refinement. At present,

they can be more rhetorical than useful.
- There is a lack of research on what constitutes a good match and whether this makes a clear difference to outcomes. We are better at knowing what broad parental characteristics are contra-indicated in approving adoptive parents, but know much less about which characteristics are best at addressing which needs the children have.
- The assessment of children's needs requires a more systematic approach and more training, not only in assessing specific needs, but also in putting these more broadly in the context of the child's development. Training in child development and in assessment has often been lacking in social work.
- Matching on ethnicity is a difficult and contentious area. Not only is more research urgently needed, but also much more attention should be paid to ways of providing inputs to a child's understanding of his or her ethnic background and ethnic identity, especially since most minority ethnic placements are of children of mixed heritage.
- Matching should be seen as part of the ecology of the development of the child in which revised assessments of needs and flexible and targeted support are part of the normal expected process of adoption. Matching should be seen as an ongoing process and not just as something that happens when or before a placement starts.
- Research priorities include the need for systematic assessment and measurement without being prescriptive about the ways in which categories might be derived from data. Straightforward accounts of practice together with some simple counts of success and failure would be useful.
- There is also a need for prospective comparative studies of planned long-term foster care versus adoption, and much more sophisticated studies of adoptions within and across ethnicities, especially on the issues of identity and the ability to cope with racism.

Preliminaries

This review is about the matching of children to families[1] in adoption, the intentions behind this process, the beliefs and principles on which this is based, and the evidence on its effectiveness. In this, intentions, beliefs and principles far outstrip the evidence.

This is partly because matching tries to put parents who have unique characteristics and capacities together with children who have particular and unique needs, whereas research usually tells us about consistencies, averages and probabilities across groups of children and parents.

Nevertheless, matching is based on information of one kind or another, whether this be research findings, descriptive accounts of practice, the unwritten discussions between practitioners themselves on their successes and failures ("practice wisdom"), or on common human judgements and hunches.

The task of summarising what we know about matching would be formidable even if the task were confined to information of this kind. But there is more to it than that, because beliefs and judgements about what is right, which cannot be settled by information alone, feed into the process as well. This is most evident in the problem of matching on ethnicity versus what are still often called "transracial"[2] placements. Deciding on the appropriateness of matching when this is the case involves more than just looking for measurable differences in placement stability or psychosocial outcomes. Such placements, in

---

1 It is a problem to decide how to refer to children and adopters at different stages in the adoption process. Terms like "adoptees", "potential adopters" and "permanent substitute parents" can become wordy and tedious. The terms "children" and "parents" are used throughout this report, except when some variety is needed, or when other terms are necessary for the sake of clarity. The children's biological parents are always referred to as "birth parents" or "birth families".

2 Terms placed within double quotation marks are contested or require some conceptual exploration. They are discussed in Chapter 3.

addition, raise the issue of whom the child "belongs to" in a cultural sense, and what a proper outcome in relation to his or her "heritage" would be.

To be sure, research and practice evidence are often brought into this, especially around the issue of a child's "identity", that is, his or her identification with the heritage from which he or she is judged to have come. But the appeal to "evidence" does not exhaust the issue; the question of whom the child belongs to culturally remains, even when the evidence has been examined. These issues are discussed in more detail in Chapter 6.

Key issues that will run through this report are:

- That the existing evidence and research activity on the effectiveness of matching is *very* thin.
- That practice works with many beliefs and assumptions that are hard to test.
- That there are aspects to matching that cannot be settled by appeals to evidence on their own.

The key questions are:

- What do we mean by children's needs?
- What do we mean by parental capacities?
- What is involved in matching on ethnicity and heritage?
- What should be looked at in terms of "outcomes", and when?
- What kind of research is needed?

Chapter 1 reviews the way in which matching is set out in policy and practice documents. Chapter 2 gives a summary of the history of matching. In Chapter 3 the concepts current in recent discussions are examined, and the methodological issues in learning more about matching are set out. Chapter 4 discusses children's "needs" and what we know about them from research, and Chapter 5 does the same for "parenting capacities". Chapter 6 outlines the research evidence on ethnic and cultural matching, and discusses what light the research throws on some contentious elements in this. Chapters 7 and 8 deal briefly with the assessment of parents and children, and Chapter 9 comments on the matching process. The final chapter considers the question of outcomes, summarises the conclusions and makes some suggestions about future research.

The limits to this review

This report is a review of *concepts and research evidence* in relation to matching. It is not a comprehensive review of the literature on adoption and permanent placements or of opinions or advice on practice where these are currently un-researched. Nor is it a review of unpublished accounts of practice, nor a survey of current practice approaches.[3] This review is restricted to a discussion of the implications of the conceptual framework surrounding matching and to a summary of the ways in which research can help in taking the matching enterprise forward.

---

3 A survey of current practice approaches is given in the recent study by Dance *et al* (2010) *Linking and Matching: A survey of adoption agency practice in England and Wales*, London: BAAF.

1   Matching in current policy and practice documents

The current emphasis on matching

The idea and purposes of matching have gone through many changes over the past 150 or more years (see Chapter 2). Currently, the process is intended to maximise the chance of finding parents who have the "capacities" to meet children's "needs". This emphasis is relatively new. It is associated with the acceptance of the "welfare principle" in the Children Act 1989, where one of the principles in the "welfare checklist" requires the court to consider 'how capable each of his parents, and any other person in relation to whom the court considers the question to be relevant, is of meeting his needs' (Section 1 (1)).

The current emphasis on matching is driven by two other pressures: the desire to lower adoption breakdown (disruption) rates, and the need to make the most of the scarce resource that is the pool of people willing to consider adopting children from care. Disruption rates following introductions and during the first year of placement are high (Rushton, 2003a), and it is thought that better approaches to matching might reduce these.

The quality of the evidence

Given this effort you might think that there is, by now, good evidence to support the idea of matching and how to do it. That is, that we would know something about how often a good match is achieved and that it makes a difference to the outcomes for the child. It is, therefore, surprising to find that such research evidence is lacking – not just sparse, but virtually absent in the UK and US literature. There are many studies on the factors related to success or failure – especially breakdown – of adoptions, but nothing on matching itself. When this report was originally written in 2006, research on "matching" was not referenced on the US Evan B. Donaldson Adoption Institute's research database, and did not occur as a topic in the index of a UK bibliography of family placement literature (Sudbery *et al*, 2005). There are many accounts and much advice on matching on the internet, but it is only recently that research on matching has been published (Dance *et al*, 2010).

Matching in current legal and policy documents

The Adoption and Children Act 2002 and the Adoption Guidance set out the legislative and practice framework (Department for Education, 2011a). The Act followed the objectives of the New Labour Government to bring 'adoption back into the mainstream of social services' (Performance and Innovation Unit, 2000). The revised Guidance takes the broad objectives of these policies forward but with some significant changes in emphasis (Department for Education, 2011a).

The overriding principle, set out in s.1(2) of the Act, is that 'The paramount consideration of the court or adoption agency must be the child's welfare, throughout his life'; s.1(4) requires the court and adoption agency, amongst other things, to have regard to: the child's wishes and feelings; the child's particular needs; the relationship of the child with relatives; the likely benefits of these continuing and the ability and willingness of the relatives to provide the child with a 'secure environment'; and finally, in s.1(5), that the courts and agencies should give '. . . due consideration to the child's religious persuasion, racial origin and cultural and linguistic background'. Taking these cultural factors into account is set against the question of delay, since delay itself is seen as likely to compromise a child's welfare. The Act is specific in cautioning that 'the court or adoption agency must at all times bear in mind that, in general, any delay in coming to a decision is likely to prejudice the child's welfare' (s.1(3)).

This last consideration inevitably leads matching away from the search for the ideal family towards the idea of a "good enough" one. This was explicitly set out in the National Adoption Standards (Adoption and Permanence Taskforce, 2004). Standard 2.2 stated that 'children are matched with adopters who best meet their assessed needs' but that 'where the child cannot be matched with a family which reflects their ethnic origin, cultural background, religion and language, the adoption agency makes every effort to find an alternative suitable family within a realistic timescale to ensure the child is not left waiting indefinitely in the care system'.

Dissatisfaction with the interpretation of this advice and the perpetuation of delays in adoption, especially of children from minority ethnic backgrounds, has led the Coalition Government to take a much stronger position on this in the revised Adoption Guidance (Department for Education, 2011a). Chapter 4 paragraph 4 states, in highlighted text, that: '*If the prospective adopter can meet most of the child's needs, the social worker must not delay placing a child with the prospective adopter because they are single, older than other adopters or does not share the child's racial or cultural background.*' The new National Minimum Standards (Department for Education, 2011b) are explicit in the requirement to look for adopters who can '. . . meet the majority, if not all, of the child's needs as set out in the Child's Permanence Report' (standard 13.4). The requirement to try to reflect the child's 'ethnic origin, cultural background, religion and language' no longer appears in the standards.

This position has been reinforced by the Parliamentary Under-Secretary of State for Children and Families (Tim Loughton MP) and from the Secretary of State for Education (Rt. Hon. Michael Gove MP), who said in a speech at the Thomas Coram Museum on 22 February 2011:

> *Thousands of children are currently in the care system waiting to be adopted. Every day they wait is a day they're denied the loving home all children deserve. But politically correct attitudes and ridiculous bureaucracy keep many of those children waiting far too long. Edicts which say children have to be adopted by families with the same ethnic background and which prevent other families adopting because they don't fit left-wing prescriptions are denying children the love they need.* (Department for Education, 2011c)

Other important features of the Guidance are referred to in later chapters. The Guidance deals mostly with regulations and procedures. It does not include advice on practice and on the philosophy that underlies the translation of the Guidance into practice. This may be because matters of practice are seen as best left to the expertise of practitioners, a position reinforced by Munro's recent reviews of child protection, which advocate a move away from the target and "tick-box" culture, to one in which social workers' professionalism is given greater freedom (Munro, 2010, 2011).

However, two documents relevant to matching are recommended as practice aids. Both of these were written during the previous administration and contain elements of and references to approaches and philosophies that may be revised (e.g. Every Child Matters and the Integrated Children's System).

The two recommended documents are outlined below, insofar as their content is relevant to matching, but first the relevant sections of the Guidance will be discussed.

The adoption Guidance

The Statutory Guidance (Department for Education, 2011a) is pre-dominantly concerned with the processes of adoption and the duties of agencies towards adopters, adopted people and birth families under the Adoption Agencies Regulations. Chapter 4 is concerned with matching and proposing a placement. Here (4.3), it is made clear that an agency should begin to identify a suitable adoptive family before a decision for adoption has been made and/or *before* consent to place-ment has been given or a placement order obtained.

The Guidance then sets out clearly the reasons that are considered to be unacceptable when rejecting potential adopters. The succinct statement on this is quoted above: i.e. potential adopters who can meet *most* of the child's needs should not be rejected because they are single, older than other adopters, or of a different ethnic background. There are no explicit references in this section to potential adopters' sexual orientation.

The Guidance makes no specific recommendations on the assess-ment of "needs", "parental capacities" and the matching process. The question of assessing needs has the potential to raise some difficulties. For example, phrases such as 'most of the child's needs' raise questions both about the hierarchy of needs (which are the most important needs or which should be met immediately) and about the assessment of them. Thus, if there is an assessed need for ethnic similarities between the adopters and the adopted child, how important is this seen to be for the welfare of the child? This is not just an academic question, but is likely to be a major issue in the adoption of older minority ethnic children. Of course, having a "loving family" is very important, but it is easy for the appeal to this to seem like an echo of the beliefs about adoption that held sway before the challenges of parenting the maltreated children, who now form the great majority of those adopted from care, became apparent.

Preparing and assessing prospective adopters

Some of these issues around assessment were considered in the advice from the then Department for Education and Skills (DfES) in *Preparing and Assessing Prospective Adopters* (2006). This deals with the requirements under the law and regulations, sets assessment and preparation firmly within the objectives of *Every Child Matters*, and takes practitioners through the process of preparation and assessment. This goes from 'information and counselling', through 'checks and references', 'adoption preparation', the assessment process, 'assessing adoptive parenting capacity', 'assessing family and environmental factors', and 'the adoption perspective'.

This is a well-written and helpful document. However, it touches only briefly on children's needs. When it gives advice on training it emphasises the origins of attachment problems, separation and loss, contact needs and, last of all, basic child development (p. 6). These "needs" are taken up in the discussion of assessing parenting capacity in Chapter 5, which also discusses emotional warmth, stimulation, guidance and boundaries and the need for stability; that is, features of parenting required by *all* children. The document also discusses the assessment of family and environmental factors – the third side of the assessment triangle in the Assessment Framework (DH, DfES and Home Office, 2000) – and also places a welcome emphasis on assessing the quality of the potential adopters' relationship.

Emphasis is placed on the potential value of using instruments and tests from the recommended list of assessment instruments (Department of Health, 2002b), as well as interview instruments that require training and skills not likely to be included in social work training, such as the Attachment Style Interview (Bifulco *et al*, 2002) or the Adult Attachment Interview (Kaniuk *et al*, 2004).

It is not yet clear how much of this advice will remain in favour. A cursory scan of documents from local authorities shows that the Assessment Framework and the related Integrated Children's System (ICS) (Department of Health, 2002a) still form the basis of assessment, but whether the use of assessment instruments – which has never been great – remains part of the recommended approach to assessment is not known, especially in the current move away from "tick boxes". The advice given in this document is discussed further in Chapter 7.

Practice guidance on assessing the support needs of adoptive families

This document (Department for Children, Schools and Families (DCSF), 2008) concerns the assessment of *support* needs of adopters and adopted children, and also the importance of working with birth families to assess the child's needs. It sets out the approach to assessing needs developed in the Assessment Framework and illustrated by the well-known assessment triangle. The report therefore provides a useful and more detailed summary of the ground covered in *Preparing and Assessing Prospective Adopters*. The use of assessment tools (*The Family Pack of Questionnaires and Scales*) is seen to bring an evidence-based approach to assessment, using a range of standardised instruments for interviewing children and families and assessing their needs. This topic is discussed further in Chapters 7 and 8.

Permanence planning: notes for practitioners

This document (Adoption and Permanence Taskforce, 2004)[4] gives advice on what should be taken into account in order to increase the chance that placements achieve permanence, and thus reflects charac-

---

4   This document is still available on the SCIE website (www.scie-socialcareonline. org.uk/repository/adoption/section08.asp) and is outlined here for this reason.

teristics of the child and the parents relevant to matching, although the direct advice on matching covers only three short pages. This advice follows an outline of two currently popular theories in child welfare: attachment and resilience. Assessment is seen to require multi-agency co-operation and should record the views and wishes of the child, all those with parental responsibility, the current carer and the children's guardian.

The advice on matching lists 12 aspects of the child and his/her circumstances that should be taken into account. This list is also based on the Assessment Framework and includes such things as: health, education, emotional and behavioural development, and the child's capacity to make new attachments. The list is considered further in Chapter 4 of the document.

A similar list is provided concerning the assessment of parents' capacities including: their experiences of being parented; how realistic their expectations of the child are; their capacity to manage the child's difficulties; and their capacity to use support appropriately. The document advises that it would be helpful in assessing families to use the dimension of "parenting capacity" as set out as part of the assessment triangle. Parenting capacities are considered in more detail in Chapter 5 of the document.

The specific advice on matching makes three further points important to the matching process. First, it is important to give applicants as much information as possible, so that they can make an informed judgement about whether they feel they 'can meet the child's needs throughout childhood and beyond'. Second, it is important not to place children who do not correspond to the profile for which the parents have been approved or expressed a preference, because this "stretching" is a predictor of placement disruption. And finally, 'it can be helpful to identify the messages that life has thus far given to this child, as these can be critical factors in matching children with the right family, such as: "I can't trust adults, they just let me down", or "In our family girls don't matter", or "I have to look after my mum when she is drunk".'

When all this has been assessed, the proposed "match" should be set out in a matching/linking report, which "needs to" give: the reasons for believing the prospective carers have the potential to meet the child's needs; the health and educational facilities which exist in the prospective carer's locality to meet the needs of the child; the preparation the prospective family has received to equip them to meet the child's needs; the views of any children or other adults in the carer's household and the nature of any preparation work which has been/needs to be carried out with them in respect of the proposed placement; how far the needs and expectations of the prospective adoptive parents would be met by the proposed placement; and further work which is necessary before and after the placement, by whom, with timescales for completion.

Finally, a *placement and adoption support plan* should set out how particular needs are to be addressed should the applicants be unable to meet them, as well as the frequency of social work visits, the type and frequency of indirect and direct contact arrangements and the worker responsible for arranging and reviewing them.

The Knowledge Review

One other helpful document is Rushton's *Knowledge Review* for SCIE on the adoption of looked after children (Rushton, 2003a). This report provides a succinct overview of current research knowledge on adoption. Perhaps for this reason, the section on matching is very brief. It notes that the Hadley Centre concluded that research has yet to provide clear indicators of what constitutes a good match. The report also raises the issue of trans-ethnic placements, an issue that is discussed in Chapter 6.

Summary

The idea of matching parental capacities to children's needs, a central feature of the Welfare Principle set out in the Children Act 1989, is now firmly part of policy and practice. It is hard to argue with the general tenor and content of the advice given to practitioners on what to take into account when undertaking this task. On the other hand, many of the characteristics of children and potential parents that should be taken into account are not well defined, their assessment is not yet part of social work training, and cannot be assessed in advance of the parents and children coming together (Cousins, 2003). The process of assessment is undergoing some innovative changes at present but is still dominated by a process that assesses needs and capacities separately.

Strangely, given the emphasis now placed on the matching process, it is striking that the word itself does not occur that frequently in official documents, and when it does, the requirements and advice concern procedures and processes, not how to match, which appears to be seen as a matter for the social work profession. The documents outlined in this chapter set out some general principles viewed as important in promoting children's welfare in permanence planning. As yet, however, they do not give pointers on how these might be translated into practice.

2 The history of "matching"

Chapter 1 has outlined how the current use of the term "matching" means the process of finding parents who have the "capacities" to meet the "needs" of the children. It is useful briefly to review how the purpose of matching has been viewed in the past, in order to remind us that the impetus behind it is located in ideas about the place of children in society, not simply in ideas of what is "best for the child". These ideas are closely related to the purposes for which the placing of children with parents or families other than their birth parents has been used. Triseliotis *et al* (1997) and Benet (1976) have provided valuable summaries of six phases or periods in the purpose and legal recognition of these practices.

A child as inheritor
In the first phase, reflected in Greek and Roman law, the purpose of adoption was closely linked to inheritance and was, therefore, designed to serve the needs of the adopters: the purpose of adoption was to provide an heir, a principle which influenced the Napoleonic Civil Code.

A child for a job
In the second phase, both in Britain and the US, finding family homes was related to the desire to provide security for orphaned and illegitimate children, with the children trading domestic or farm labour for security. Poor children and those from poorhouses or almshouses were indentured to families who were supposed to care for, educate and train them in response to their work for the family. Indenture was one of the principal ways in which children were placed in families.

At the same time, there were developments in both the UK and the US to board out children from urban regions into rural areas, partly to provide a source of free labour for poor Scottish crofters and for farmers in the American West. Amongst the most famous of these movements were the orphan trains in the US. Between 1854 and 1929, as many as 250,000 children from New York and other eastern cities were sent by train to towns in mid-western and western states, as well as to Canada and Mexico. Families interested in the orphans came to look them over when they were placed on display in local train stations, and placements were frequently made with little or no investigation or oversight. However, these movements of children did not usually separate children from their birth families permanently (University of Oregon, The Adoption History Project).

In the US, these placements could turn into something akin to adoption, which might be legalised through specific acts of legislature (Witmer, 1963) but in Britain they remained without legal security. Adopted children were expected to work hard, behave well and be grateful to the families who took them in.

Care for destitute children and orphans

By the middle of the nineteenth century these policies were being overwhelmed by the numbers of destitute children in institutions, whose plight led to demands for better care. This pressure coincided with religious revivalism in the second half of the century and to the opening, by religious groups or individual philanthropists, of large orphanages and institutions to care for the children. These institutions themselves often had serious problems with infant mortality, and this led to further attempts to place these children with families.

The legal regularisation of adoption in the US began in Massachusetts in 1851 and included the requirements that a judge be satisfied that the adoption was 'fit and proper'. This went along with the legal and complete severance of the relationship between the child and the biological parents (Kadushin and Martin, 1988).

In Britain, the first adoption law was not passed until 1926, the reasons for the delay being: first, the stigma attached to illegitimacy and fears that the children might inherit the "bad traits" of their parents; second, the guarding by the courts of parents' rights; third, the reluctance to see the family inheritance pass to outsiders; and finally, the maintenance of class lines based on kinship (Costin *et al*, 1991; Triseliotis, 1995). When the law was finally passed the courts, as in the US, emphasised the need for judicial supervision for the protection of the child.

In the US between the wars, infant adoptions gained in popularity, influenced by the drop in the birth rate following World War I, the influenza epidemic of 1918, the development of artificial feeding for infants, and the growing perception of the importance of the early environment (Sokoloff, 1993). In both the US and the UK during this period, a number of agencies were set up to facilitate adoptions. In the US, especially, there was a continuing emphasis on the welfare of the child and the need to investigate prospective adoptive homes.

However, it should be noted that these early concerns about the welfare of the child focused predominantly on the need to protect the child from harm and exploitation. It did not include an assumption that something active needed to be done to promote the child's psychosocial development. Indeed, this notion did not come into play in a serious way until the most recent period – a "family for developmental recovery" (see below). Meanwhile, in both this and the next phase, notions from eugenics continued to influence ideas on who was adoptable.

A child for a home

In the third phase – following World War II – the motivation for adoption changed to that of a solution for infertility. During this period the emphasis was on finding the "perfect baby" for the "perfect couple", with great efforts being put into matching children to parents in order to create a family as much like the biological one as possible – including matching on looks. During this period an adoptable infant was generally thought to be white, healthy and developing normally. Parents were subject to extensive investigations, guided by psychoanalytic theory, to assess their capacity as parents. Generally, also, the religion of the adopting family had to match that of the infant, a principle emphasised by religiously-based adoption agencies and related to the modern concern of preserving a culture or heritage.

By the late 1960s, almost three-quarters of the children adopted by non-relatives in Britain and in the US were under one year old, with a substantial proportion of the supply of adoptable babies coming from the "illegitimate" offspring of young women who were often pressured into giving them up. Children who were older or who had even minor disabilities were likely to be raised in institutions. The feature of this period was "a child for a home" and parents' needs seemed paramount, despite the legal emphasis on protecting the interests of the child.

A home for a child

In the fourth phase, which began in the mid-1960s in response to the dramatic decline in the number of babies available for adoption, social services took on an increasingly important role. At this time, revelations about the numbers of children languishing in institutions or drifting through unstable foster placements highlighted the need to do something for what have come to be known as "special needs" children, that is, those who are not infants, may have disabilities of a physical or psychosocial kind, may be of minority ethnic heritage or of mixed ethnicity parentage, or have siblings who also need placement.

Despite the increasing focus on children with problematic early experiences and special needs, this phase was not marked by the view that special parental capacities and supports were needed to help children to get over the hardships they had suffered. Rather, the idea was the general one that the love of adoptive parents would be sufficient to achieve this, a view finding an echo in the most recent official thinking (Department for Education, 2011c).

A family for developmental recovery

This final phase, which I have called "a family for developmental recovery", has brought together the change in the population of children seen to need the permanence of adoption, and the growing evidence on what is needed to help them overcome the effects of often severe maltreatment. In the previous phase, there was a broad assumption that the placement of a "special needs" child in a stable family would in itself provide the environment in which the child could return to a normal developmental trajectory. In this most recent phase, it has been recognised that this is often not the case, rather that the effects of early maltreatment are often marked in their expression, persistent over time, and increase the risk that an adoption will not succeed.

The instability of some placements and the persistence of difficulties, which are of course related, have brought us to the current emphasis on matching children's needs to parents' capacities, rather than simply on finding a child for a family or a family for a child. Matching, then, does not just mean "live with and tolerate" the problems and issues a child may bring to a placement. It is also intended to make a difference to the level of those difficulties. How these needs and capacities are conceptualised is the subject of Chapters 4 and 5.

Summary

Adoption and other forms of permanent family placement have been used for a variety of purposes over time, but it is only recently that its primary purpose has shifted to promoting the welfare of children through trying to provide what they need to overcome the effects of severe early hardships and maltreatment. This is very different from earlier attempts at matching, which were primarily concerned to find children who would look like the families they entered or to preserve religious affiliations. Placement itself was seen as sufficient to deal with the welfare issue. It is only in the most recent phase that matching as a way of meeting the welfare objective has been advanced, especially in terms of specifying the developmental needs of the child and what might be needed to address these. The next four chapters discuss how the elements of the matching process are conceptualised and put into practice.

3   Some key terms and conceptual issues

In this chapter some of the principal terms used in discussions and documents on matching are considered. Many of these terms are dealt with more fully in later chapters, for example, "needs", "capacities" and "ethnicity", but some general discussion of their meaning is useful at this point.

In none of the policy or practice literature have these general terms been closely or carefully defined. Instead, they are used to reflect overall intentions, without going into detail on what might be meant by them. It may just be a matter of preference or pedantry to be concerned about this; maybe we all know what we mean by "needs", "capacities", "race" and "ethnicity" and ought to be content to leave it at that. On the other hand, the lack of clarity may get in the way of effective assessment and decision-making and therefore be against the welfare of children. Lack of clarity also makes it difficult to research the issue, to learn more about what makes a good match and to increase our knowledge of the matching process. Lack of clarity, or at least lack of good definitions, may be one reason why there is so little research on the effectiveness of matching.

Matching

In current usage, the term "matching" describes the process through which potential adopters are identified, with the intention of finding those who have the "parenting capacities" to meet the "needs" of specific children. Matching should be distinguished from *family recruitment*, the process of assembling a pool of potential adopters for whom matched children are sought, and *family finding*, the process of identifying several families from such a pool who might match with a particular child. The broad assessment of parenting capacities is a part of these two processes.

The welfare of the child is seen as the paramount objective in the process of matching. Legislation, guidance and regulations do not go beyond this general prescription. This apparently clear aim conceals a number of challenging questions, even if we can make progress on the definitions. The first question is whether the endeavour makes any difference: is putting a lot of effort into "matching" worth it? Of course, we need to assess the general suitability of potential adopters, but we probably know enough about the characteristics required already. How much more specific do we need to be in matching parents' capacities to children's needs? Is it better to look for a broad range of parental skills and attributes, or should we be trying to match specific capacities to specific needs?

To understand these questions we need to decide what we mean by "needs" and "capacities" and how we should assess them. We then need to learn which capacities will meet which needs and how we might know whether achieving a match on these has made a difference. In this, there is likely to be a question of priorities: which needs should we pay attention to first or consider more important than others? This last question bears especially on the problems of matching on ethnicity, where the search for a match may be in conflict with minimising delay, and therefore in conflict with the welfare principle.

Children's needs

The conceptualisation of "children's needs" is considered in more detail in Chapter 4. At this juncture, it should be noted that current usage has become broader than that in the Children Act 1989, where a child was deemed to be "in need" if he or she had a disability or was, or was likely to be, disadvantaged in health or social, intellectual, emotional or behavioural development *if a service were not forthcoming*[5] (III) (17)(10). Thus, the term was a 'legal term of art' (Allen, 1992), a restricted definition of need tied to the notion of some disadvantage remediable by a service. Logically, this has the curious consequence that if a child has a problem for which there is no known effective intervention, then the child could not be deemed to be "in need".

In the US literature, the term "special needs" has a still more

---

5 Emphasis added

restricted meaning and is used to refer to children who are hard to place, for example, if they are aged three or older, of minority ethnic or mixed-race heritage ("children of color"), or part of a sibling group (McKenzie, 1993; Rosenthal, 1993). Of course, a much broader range of needs are taken into account when placing children.

The use of the term "need" in current discussions in the UK is broader than in the Children Act, although a residue of the service-based definition remains in the idea of "children in need" and in the idea that needs should be "met". The service-based definition is also reflected in the Assessment Framework, where the assessment of needs goes along with the assessment of "parenting capacities" and a judgement on appropriate service responses. What was new in the Assessment Framework was the introduction of the idea of making systematic assessments of development in seven areas drawn from developmental psychology, together with recommendations on the use of standard measures to help in assessing these (Department of Health, 2000).

Other discussions of meeting children's needs go beyond this objective of addressing psychosocial difficulties. In a variety of documents, including the BAAF assessment forms, the needs that ought to be met include things that might come under a heading of "quality of life" or "respect for the child as a person", regardless of whether meeting these "needs" has developmental implications. For example, paying attention to a child's wishes and feelings is likely to reveal "wants" as well as "needs".

It is, of course, right and proper to respect children and to pay attention to their wishes and feelings, regardless of whether there will be negative developmental implications if we do not. On the other hand, this applies to our treatment of *all* children, adopted or otherwise. It is thus important in the assessment of applicants who want to adopt, but is not specific to the matching process.

"Meeting" needs

In dictionary definitions, the word 'meet' has meanings that range from 'come together by chance or arrangement', through 'assemble for a particular purpose', to 'fulfil or satisfy'. It seems clear that this last meaning is what is intended in the literature on matching, but, in practice, putting together children and new parents is likely to reflect all these shades of meaning, including, indeed, 'come together for a contest', depending on the skill or luck in matching and the working of unforeseeable influences. Practice advice is silent on how we might know whether a need has been satisfied.

Again, this is not just a question of being pernickety about meanings. How we understand the notion of "meeting needs" will make a difference to what we consider to be a good match, and how, in the longer run, we will decide whether we were right. For example, do we decide that a match is good on the basis of the perceived adequacy of our matching, or do we wait for a while to see if problems diminish or disappear? If problems stay at the same level even though adopters are trying their best, do we decide that they have met the child's needs or not? Do we try to come to some judgement on whether the outcome is the best that we might expect?

For these reasons, the notion of "meeting" needs can be prob-lematic. It carries with it a high promise for a child's welfare associated with only a vague notion of how we would know if we had succeeded. Maybe no one really expects needs to be met in a narrow sense. Rather, the sub-text may be something more prosaic like: "work actively to help" or "address", or "cope as well as might be reasonably expected". The term "meet" is now firmly entrenched in policy and practice, but we need to admit that the narrow objective of meeting a need so that the need no longer exists may often be unachievable.

Parental capacities

Children's needs are now linked in policy and practice to parents' "capacities" to meet them. The Oxford English Dictionary definitions of "capacity" include: 'ability to take in or hold', 'ability to take in impressions, ideas, knowledge', and 'the power, ability or faculty for anything in particular'. Parenting abilities on any or all of these meanings nicely fit what one might be looking for in potential adopters, although the definitions also carry the implication that capacities have their limits, that someone or something may be operating at "full capacity". Moreover, assessing people's capacities before they are put to the test is possible only in a very broad sense.

Outcomes

The dispiriting lack of evidence on the effectiveness of matching itself has been pointed out. Most of the research that is of use comes from studies that take adoption disruption[6] as their measure of outcome. This is true both for parenting capacities – where most studies report on rather broad features of parental characteristics, and much less frequently on parenting *behaviours* – and for children's needs, where the majority of studies are concerned with the characteristics and behaviours that lead to termination. These studies are summarised in Chapters 4 and 5.

Here, the general issue of what we might mean by "outcomes" is considered. This is important to matching, since deciding whether a child's needs have been met depends on having adequate outcome assessments. That is, if we take "meeting" to imply fulfilling or satisfying needs, then we need to be clear about how that might be judged. This is not just a question of measurement, although without that we simply cannot know where we are unless we are prepared to rely on summary opinions from practitioners reflected in such questions as: Do you think that this placement worked out: better than you expected/about as well as you expected/worse than you expected/very poorly?

In child development, the term "outcome" reflects where children have got to in their psychosocial or physical development at some point in their lives. The term is sometimes used as if it implied an end-point, that they have got as far as they are going to get, but this is not so. Developmental trajectories may change, either positively or

---

6 Recent US literature has begun to define "disruption" as breakdowns that occur before the adoption is finalised and "dissolution" for breakdowns that occur after it. The term "termination" had replaced "breakdown", which seems to be no longer used.

negatively, but to understand these some agreed and reliable methods of measurement are required if we are to make comparisons across time.

Interpreting such data, in order to come to some judgement about whether matching has worked and whether needs have been met, raises the important questions of what comparisons should be made and what it is reasonable to expect. Nearly all children currently adopted from care have had a very poor start in life and some of their resulting difficulties prove to be very resistant to change (Rushton and Dance, 2004; Selwyn *et al*, 2006). Given this, how should we judge the success of matching, beyond the simple criterion of whether the placement has lasted or not, which is not, in itself, a good indicator of psychosocial change.[7]

A variety of comparisons are possible, all of which tell us something useful about outcomes. For example, we may compare adopted children's intellectual attainment, as reflected in exam results, against that of the general school population in their area, or against children with social or educational disadvantage, or with children in other kinds of placement, such as long-term foster care, or we may compare them with themselves: that is, we can ask what progress they have made since they were placed. However, none of these assessments of outcome is possible without consistent assessment and measurement at the time of placement or before, and at the point at which "outcomes" are to be judged.

The content of such assessments needs careful thought. It should include reliable measures of health and educational attainment as well as standard assessments of "mental health".[8] There also needs to be some assessment of attachment disorders, even though the definition

---

7   For example, Rushton and Dance's follow-up of 130 adoptions made under the age of ten to age 16, found that about a third of intact adoptions were, nevertheless, experiencing persistent problems (2004).

8   "Mental health" is used to cover the standard classifications of emotional and behavioural problems, including conduct and oppositional disorder, anxiety and depression, attention deficit/hyperactivity disorder (ADHD) as well as eating disorders and rarer conditions such as obsessive/compulsive disorder and autism (Meltzer *et al*, 2000, 2003).

and measurement of these is not well established (O'Connor and Zeanah, 2003). Beyond these we come into more contested territory. Here, the outcomes might include "self-esteem" and "identity" (Quinton, 2006), both of which terms are commonly mentioned in discussions of the outcomes for looked after and adopted children but for whom adequate measures are difficult to devise.

Race, ethnicity, culture and heritage

Debates about definitions, terms and underlying beliefs about race and ethnicity have been fierce, and the topic remains a contested and contentious area of study. The concept of "race" remains in official use as well as in common parlance, despite critiques of its biological usefulness (Koenig *et al*, 2008). This is partly due to the inertia of legal and other systems where a term becomes perpetuated once it has been written into laws and procedures. Thus we had the Commission for Racial Equality, set up in 1976, which only became part of the broader Equality and Human Rights Commission in 2007.

In adoption, the matching process is required by law to '. . . give due consideration to the child's religious persuasion, racial origin and cultural and linguistic background' (Adoption and Children Act, 2002 s.1(5)), even though the emphasis placed on this in regulations and guidance has changed (see above). Attempts to match on these characteristics have to be balanced against the negative effects of delay, should the time take to match on them prove too long. It might be thought that these concepts are well defined and that a clearly understood set of meanings were attached to them by those who drafted and approved the legislation, but this does not seem to be the case.

There is clear evidence that practitioners take this matter seriously, but no official guidance attempts a definition of these broad terms, so practitioners are left to their own experience, presumptions and practice pressures in making decisions. Some discussion of these topics is appropriate here.

Race

The idea of sorting humans into distinct "races" arose in the eighteenth and nineteenth centuries in the context of European colonial domination and the development of scientific classifications of the natural world. The latter involved the hierarchical ordering of plants and animals into groups based on *differences*, as in the idea of species and sub-species. In the twentieth century, these classifications of peoples based on physical type linked them with specific geographical areas, so that the idea of "race" came to involve physical distinctness – most commonly skin tone – and an associated area of geographical origin. It thus united two features of "otherness": that a group is physically distinguishable and comes from somewhere else (Marks, 2008). This meaning is still apparent in current usage and belief.

Recently, the idea that this otherness is something immutable or "essential" has been linked to a misreading of the genetics of inheritance, even though, as Lewontin pointed out as long ago as 1972, it is not possible to specify a set of defining genes for race (Lewontin, 1972). Indeed, the amount of genetic variation within supposedly similar populations ("races") is greater than that between different ones (see also Dupre, 2008).[9]

The use of the term "race" appears to be in decline in the UK amongst professionals concerned with adoption, but is still common in the US where it is often distinguished, in an unspecific way, from ethnicity. Its use had become further complicated in relation to medical practice, especially pharmacology related to "race" (see several articles in Koenig *et al*, 2008).

The predominant view amongst geneticists and sociologists is that the term "race" is a social construction that is not biologically meaningful. Rather, as Haslanger has observed (2008), the use of the term reflects relationships of power, domination and oppression, through which a group can be treated differentially in economic and social ways because of '. . . observed or imagined bodily features presumed

---

9   It should be pointed out that this is still a matter of technical debate within population genetics. See Edwards, 2003; Witherspoon *et al*, 2007.

to be evidence of an ancestral link to a certain geographic region'. The continued use of the term in social policy and political discussions seems appropriate *only* when it refers to abuses of power and to actions deriving from *mistaken* beliefs about essential differences. That is, when it refers to "racism".

A contrary argument is put forward by some sociologists (Ifekwunigwe, 2004), who argue that the term should be retained because the identities of individuals from minority ethnic groups become "racialised" through the prejudiced views of the majority ethnic grouping. The problem with this argument is that adopting it is likely to perpetuate a belief in differences that is not helpful in child welfare.

Ethnicity

Although "race" is still used in discussions on child placement, there has been a general move to replace it with the term "ethnicity", because this potentially avoids the trap of essentialist arguments and takes language, religion and social and family patterns into account. The features that differentiate ethnicities often go along with differences in physical appearance, but physical characteristics need not be part of the definition of ethnicity. Ethnicity always involves relationships and contacts between people who are seen to be different, as well as between those who are seen to be the same. A sense of ethnicity can only arise in the context of relationships and interaction with others. Defining *us* implies an image of *them*.

However, because of the association of ethnicity with physical differences, the term can itself easily become an acceptable proxy for "race", as can other alternatives such as "ancestry" or "heritage", and thus retain essentialist elements. Even when "ethnicity" is used without these undertones, it can still be accompanied by mistaken ideas that an ethnic culture is both homogeneous and unchanging. As Modood and his colleagues have pointed out, there are no satisfactory terms for referring to black, Asian and mixed ethnicity children as a group, because they are so diverse in physical and cultural heritage (Modood *et al*, 1997). That ethnicity may be negotiable, flexible, and variable in its significance from one situation to another is among the most important lessons of the specialist social science literature (Cornell, 1996), but when ethnicity matters to people it can move them to action and awaken powerful emotions.

There are additional problems in defining a child's "ethnicity" when it comes to matching on it. These problems are not just ones of ignorance, such as classifying all those with family origins in the Indian sub-continent or the Far East as "Asians", but also problems arising from assuming that birth parents are equally attached to all aspects of their ethnicity. This problem arises because of mistaken assumptions about the homogeneity of cultures. In practice, many parenting characteristics vary much more within cultures than between them (Quinton, 1994), a fact that applies to genetic variation as well (Long and Kittles, 2003).

These problems are compounded when children are considered to be of "mixed ethnicity" where the "mixture" itself reflects a departure from simple notions of ethnic coherence. This is not a small problem in matching, since 75 per cent of "minority ethnic" children for whom placements were recently sought through the Adoption Register were of "mixed heritage", commonly "white" mothers and fathers from a minority ethnic group (Adoption Register for England and Wales, 2010).

Despite these concerns, research, policy and practice need some way of referring to the children with these backgrounds, even though the limitations of all descriptive labels, especially in aggregate, are obvious. "Ethnicity" and "ethnic minority" seem the least loaded terms, even though some children are not a "minority" in their own local authority areas, and also that the word "ethnic" can have negative connotations, as, for example, in the term "ethnic cleansing". Further, in everyday discourses ethnic minorities are not usually contrasted with ethnic majorities, but with the older racial category of "white". In the US the term "Caucasian", which derives from much earlier discussions of race, is still much in evidence, but is little used in the UK.

Culture

Most definitions of culture include the beliefs, conventional or approved behaviours and symbolic representations that are shared by a group of individuals, have some persistence over time, and are transmitted to new members of a society or institution. These include religious beliefs, gender relationships, patterns of power and deference, rules of inheritance, ways of dressing and social presentation, and acceptable and non-acceptable foods, etc (Quinton, 1994).

Within all societies, individuals belong to more than one social grouping, constituted with respect to age, sex, social status and other features. Each grouping will have its own "sub-culture". Individuals are active participants in the creation and maintenance of these cultures and in negotiating their own sense of themselves in relation to them.[10] That is, cultures are human processes of meaning-making. Cultures are not static and fixed. Within any group there will be individuals who do not go along with the norms and values of that culture – individuals who challenge it and behave differently (Tizard and Phoenix, 2002). Culture also shifts over time to accommodate new ways of thinking and being, so some of what has been taught is lost and new elements are added, often through contact with other cultures. Culture both embraces and resists change.

Heritage

The term "heritage" is used to refer to presumed core or key features and artefacts from the cultures of a child's parents and ancestors. To use the word usually implies that there is value in preserving these cultural features and that a child has the right to have them passed on to him or her. For mainstream society the term is commonly used to refer to historic buildings, objects, literary and artistic outputs and the like, but it is also used to refer to approved ways of behaving, often those that are presumed to have been better in the past. "Heritage" is

---

10 This discussion draws on *The Blackwell Encyclopaedia of Sociology* at www.sociologyencyclopaedia.com/public and on Bhopal, 2004.

also sometimes used as a proxy for "ethnicity", also in a nostalgic and idealised way.

In its positive sense, the term connects to the importance to individuals of a connectedness with their personal and cultural history (Owusu-Bempah, 2006). In its less positive usage, it tries to assert the importance for individual identity of taking on traditions that may have little relevance to an individual. Connections with a heritage are very variable and personal, as can be seen in programmes like the BBC's *Who do you think you are?*

Identity

Research and practice in adoption have been much concerned with the effects of adoption on an individual's "sense of identity". This is because adopted people have to come to terms with the differences between their biological origins and the families and social circum-stances in which they are reared, as Kirk pointed out long ago in his classic study *Shared Fate* (1964). This issue has been of particular concern in adoptions that cross ethnicities, but it has also been much discussed more generally, especially in terms of the consequences of contact with birth parents and families. "Identity" is often invoked as an issue without discussion of the sense in which the term is being used.[11]

Our "identity" may be thought of as a *story of ourselves* (Quinton, 2006): where we come from, where we fit into social life, to whom we are related, and so on. If we do not feel we have a coherent story of this kind, then our sense of ourselves as individuals is likely to be compromised. Identity formation can be more difficult for adopted people, not just because of the problem of solving the task outlined above, but also because of social barriers that make it hard to access information about origins and because of the ways in which their adoptive status can lead to stigmatising behaviours on the part of others (Evan B. Donaldson Adoption Institute, 2009).

---

11 For a useful summary of concepts of identity in adoption see Evan B. Donaldson Adoption Institute, 2009.

These complexities point to two different ways in which "identity" is used (Grotevant *et al*, 2000). The first involves those things that society "outside of us" thinks are important or uses as the bases for social classifications, such as a person's name, date of birth, sex, ethnicity, sexuality and other things that "identify" her or him. These have been called the 'big descriptors' (Quinton, 2006).

The second usage involves what is meant by a "sense of identity": that is, how securely does someone feel able to place herself or himself in the world; how sure are they about their personal history; and how certain and comfortable with "who I am"? There is a need to feel included in Society, the family and the social group. But in addition to this, individuals also define themselves by the things that make them *different*, like their interests or musical tastes. Tastes and identifications change over time and place and so does the individual importance of the big descriptors. Some aspects of identity, like being a child, get left behind and others have to be taken on, like being a parent. Their importance to individual identity depends on how important the individual sees them to be. These two motives are in a regular dialogue, and sometimes tension, throughout life.

There is an additional pressure on adopted individuals and their adoptive parents, especially in trans-ethnic placements. This is because of the expectation that the adopted children take on the culture and heritage of the minority ethnic families from which they come and a consequent judgement that their outcome is only satisfactory if this identification is achieved.

Summary

It is clear that the terms used in the field of matching need some conceptual clarification and, for many of them, some closer definition and specification. This is not just a matter of semantic fussiness but has implications for assessment and measurement and therefore for learning more about the matching process and its effectiveness. This is not just "research-speak" either. Unless we know where children have got to developmentally at the time of placement and whether this has changed subsequently, we will not know how to target support effectively, what that support might best be and what kinds of interventions and therapies are most likely to be effective. Questions of measurement and research strategies are considered in Chapter 10.

It is also clear from this review that the "needs" that law and practice emphasise, especially around culture and ethnicity, go beyond questions that research can effectively answer. They involve considerations of rights and beliefs as well. To insist that these needs are met does not depend on evidence of measurable benefits to psychosocial development (Quinton and Selwyn, 2006) although, if there were evidence that to insist on them were harmful, then this insistence would be in conflict with the welfare principle.

This issue raises some questions on outcome that relate to the discussion of external and personal identity outlined above. For example, is it a satisfactory or unsatisfactory outcome if a trans-ethnically placed child is happy later in life with his or her self and sense of acceptance within society but does not identify with his or her ethnic background?

The contribution of existing research to what we might conclude about children's needs, parental capacities, matching generally and matching on ethnicity in particular is the subject of the next three chapters.

4   Children's needs

The purpose of this chapter is to consider the contribution that research can make to identifying the "needs" that ought to be assessed during the process of matching, and whether it is possible to prioritise these. Some needs are already built into legislation and emphasised in the practice literature and a broad hierarchy set out concerning those that should be taken into account first. It is important to think about this since the application of these hierarchies affects decisions about which needs to address.

The hierarchy of needs in legislation

Legislation and guidance set a broad hierarchical framework for thinking about needs. At the top of the hierarchy is 'the child's welfare, throughout his life', which cannot be secured without the provision of a 'secure enviroment', usually through establishing permanence, preferentially with relatives, providing that they can address needs as well (Adoption and Children Act, s.1(4)). Although 'welfare through-out life' is not necessarily met through permanence, since a permanent placement may have features that are inimical to welfare, permanence in one form or another is a top-level aim because the objective of welfare is unlikely to be achieved without it.

On the next level there is the requirement to give '... due con-sideration to the child's religious persuasion, racial origin and cultural and linguistic background' (s.1(5)). To give 'due consideration' implies that they should be met if possible but that they can be set aside if attempts to match on them leads to delay that can be harmful to the child's overall welfare, presumably by prolonging uncertainty and preventing permanence. The most recent adoption guidance (Department for Education, 2011a) has taken the view that an emphasis on matching on ethnicity has had the serious effect of increasing delay in placement for many children.

An implication of this view is that meeting cultural needs is not *essential* to a child's welfare and that it should be set aside if to do so would, on balance, benefit the child's psychosocial development in other ways and lead more rapidly to a permanent placement. Nevertheless, some ambiguity remains in the Act since it is not clear whether 'taking these things into account' is emphasised because it is thought that failure to do so has adverse developmental consequences, or because taking them into account respects the cultural rights of the child and of his/her community, or both. In both practice advice and academic literature, taking ethnicity into account is often linked to an explicit argument about the adverse psychosocial consequences of a failure to meet this need (Triseliotis *et al*, 1997), especially with respect to identity.

Selwyn *et al*'s 2010 study is the only one to provide data from England on delays that may be related to a preference for matching on ethnicity. In this study, the likelihood of an adoptive placement being made was lower for black and Asian children compared with those of white or mixed white/minority ethnic heritage. The authors' interpretation of this was that it was related to an over-rigid application of matching rules and also to social workers' greater insecurity in decision making for these children, including a general pessimism about the likelihood of finding matched families.

Needs of other kinds are only generally mentioned in the Act (... that the court and agencies should have regard to the 'child's particular needs' (s.1(4)), but are set out in more detail in advice recommended by the Department for Education.

Recommendations for practice

Aspects of the child's life and psychosocial functioning are specified in some detail in the guidance on assessing the support needs of adoptive families (Department for Children, Schools and Families, 2008). This guidance was produced during the New Labour administration, but remains recommended at the time of writing. This list of areas that should be assessed includes: health; education; emotional and behavioural development; identity; family and social relationships; attachment history and the child's capacity to make new attachments;

the quality of the child's attachment to the current carer and the capacity of the current carer to help the child attach to a new family; contact needs; social presentation; self-care skills; accommodation and locality; and any other needs specific to the child.

This list was first set out in the Looking After Children System (LAC) (Ward, 1995), and subsequently developed in the Assessment Framework (Department of Health, Department for Education and Skills and Home Office, 2000), and taken forward into the Integrated Children's System (Cleaver *et al*, 2008). It includes areas of functioning that would rarely be problematic in families that are not "in need", such as social presentation and self-care skills. These are important inclusions, since problems in either have adverse implications for social – especially peer – relationships and the reactions of adults to the child.

This list is strongly based on understandings that come from developmental psychology and is not contentious. The broad aspects of children's development that parents think are important applies across cultural groups, as the community survey by Ward and her colleagues found (1995), although these needs will be shown differently in different cultures and there may be different views on how they should be assessed and addressed.

There seems no reason to dissent from this list, although some areas are broader than others and arguments can be raised about appropriate emphases and sub-divisions. In addition, there is considerable variation in the precision of definitions and the quality of measurement available to assess needs in these areas (see Chapter 7).

The remainder of this chapter will consider the research on adoption that might be relevant to the assessment and categorisation of children's needs. It is striking that the great majority of the studies have used adoption disruption as its outcome measure. No studies have been found that use the assessment of needs at the time of placement as predictors of outcomes. The focus on the correlates and predictors of disruption is useful in that "permanence" is a *sine qua non* of applying the welfare principle, but it is of limited use in deciding which needs to assess in the first place and how to do this or, indeed, whether it is possible to do so.

Research evidence on children's needs that are a threat to stability

Studies of disruption[12]

There are many studies on child and family factors that are related to disruption. This review is illustrative rather than exhaustive, since its purpose is to consider what might be helpful in identifying "needs" that relate to matching. There are a number of substantial reviews of this literature (Rosenthal, 1993; Evan B. Donaldson Adoption Institute, 2004). These reviews are drawn on for this overview. The few UK studies that have looked at psychosocial outcomes prospectively are considered in the next section.

Age at placement

The most consistent finding with respect to termination of adoptions is the child's age at placement: the older the child, the greater the risk. Evidence from the US for this comes from numerous studies (e.g. Barth and Berry, 1988; Berry and Barth, 1990; Smith and Howard, 1991; Rosenthal, 1993; Goerge *et al*, 1995; Berry, 1997; McRoy, 1999; Barth, 2000).

Goerge and colleagues (1995) found disruption and displacement rates to rise by age group from 12 per cent for those aged under one to 21 per cent for those aged 10–14, and 35 per cent for those aged 15 and older. Controlling for all other factors, children aged 5–9 were almost twice as likely, children 10–14 more than four times more likely, and those 15 or older nine times more likely to experience disruption than children aged under one. Triseliotis (2002) reviewed US and UK studies and summarised the findings as showing very low rates of disruption for early placements, two per cent under the age of one and about five per cent for pre-school children. After this, disruption rates rose markedly to 15 per cent for those aged 5–12 and

---

12 It was noted earlier that the US literature has abandoned the term "breakdown" and has begun further to sub-divide "disruptions" depending on when they occur in the process of adoption. For simplicity's sake, the term "disruption" is used to cover the ending of adoptive placements at any point from placement onwards.

over 33 per cent for adoptions made in adolescence.

Howe's (1997) retrospective study of the adjustment of adopted adolescents showed that markedly adverse parenting in early childhood was the key factor, rather than age on its own. Children adopted later in childhood with good early care had no more emotional and behavioural problems than those adopted in infancy, but those adopted later following poor early care showed a marked increase in difficulties. It can be concluded that disruption rises with age largely because age goes along with a number of other contributing factors. Amongst these are: the length of earlier exposure to pathogenic environments; more entrenched emotional and behavioural problems because of this; increasing difficulty in forming positive relationships with adopters, often because of loyalties to birth parents; and ambivalence about committing to new parents as the need for autonomy increases (Barth, 2000).

A history of disruptions

Many studies have concluded that disruption itself predicts future disruption (Festinger, 1986; Partridge et al, 1986; Barth et al, 1988; Groze, 1996). In his 1993 review, Rosenthal concluded that the number of prior foster placements, the time already spent in placements, and adoption delays are predictors of disruption. In Barth and Berry's study (1988), one-quarter of the children in disrupted placements had been adopted previously compared with five per cent in placements that did not disrupt. Similar associations were found by Festinger (1986), where 23 per cent of children whose placements disrupted had had previous adoptive placements, compared with only eight per cent among the group of finalised adoptions.

Barth and Berry (1988) found that the number of previous placements increased with age depending on the number of problems the child had. Festinger's (1986) disrupted group had more placements of any kind than the intact group, on average 2.71 placements for the disrupted group and 1.27 in the intact group. However, McRoy (1999) did not find a difference between her disrupted/dissolved and her intact groups in the number of previous foster care placements.

Findings are also inconsistent on whether the length of time in care previously is a predictor of disruption. Goerge and colleagues (1995) found such an association, although the findings showed a complex pattern, with disruption being greater for children who had been in care less than two or over four years, but Festinger (1986) did not. Rosenthal (1993) noted in his review that many children from disrupted adoptive placements go on to stable adoptions, a finding repeated in Selwyn *et al*'s study, *Costs and Outcomes of Non-Infant Adoptions* (2006). Most disruptions occurred during introductions or in the early stages of the placement but, even so, some children went on to stable adoptions.

It is unlikely that further examination of associations between the frequency or the length of prior placements will increase the predictive power of these factors, and thus be of use in matching, apart from raising general cautions on their value as markers for other things that might be looked for. Length of prior placement or a longer time in care may operate though different mechanisms, for example, when an adoptive placement disrupts an established relationship between the children and their foster carers. The number of placement changes may index emotional, behavioural and relationship problems that are the main influences on placement instability. Unless the reasons for changes are understood, it is not possible to make sense of associations between the number of changes and outcomes. Of course, changes themselves generate disturbance for children and may contribute to psychosocial problems.

A history of maltreatment

Understanding the influence of prior maltreatment on placement disruption and psychosocial outcomes is difficult because the majority of children placed for adoption nowadays have been maltreated in one way or another. Moreover, different types of maltreatment frequently overlap, making it even more difficult to disentangle the effects of different kinds of abuse and neglect. Perhaps for this reason, even well-sampled prospective studies frequently fail to find associations. This is true, for example, in the studies by Quinton and his colleagues (Quinton *et al*, 1998) and in Selwyn *et al*'s recent study (2006).

Several US studies have found prior sexual abuse to increase the risk of disruption (Barth and Berry, 1988; Smith and Howard, 1991; Rosenthal, 1993). Smith and Howard (1994) compared 35 sexually abused children with 113 who had no identified history of sexual abuse. The disruption rate was higher in the abused group and abuse was associated with more moves in care, greater behavioural difficulties, hostile acting out and more attachment problems. For some, the abuse intensified their difficulties in separating from birth parents; for others, the task of trusting and yielding control to their new parents brought their long-submerged trauma back to the surface.

Strikingly, the abuse was often unknown to caseworkers when the child came into care, and in many cases only became known long after the adoptive placement was made. Similarly, although about one-third of the children in Barth and Berry's study of adoption disruption (1988) had been sexually abused, less than one-half of their adoptive parents knew about the abuse at the time of placement. Over one-half of the pre-adoptive placements of these children disrupted, and the discovery of a history of sexual abuse was strongly associated with disruption (Berry, 1997). In a study in Illinois of later-placed children (after age seven) receiving post-adoption support services, pre-adoptive sexual abuse was also associated with more moves in care and was a predictor of inconsistent parental commitment and adoption disruption (Nalavany *et al*, 2008).

There has been recent interest in the phenomenon of parental *selective rejection* of children, that is, when one child is singled out and scapegoated or is actively expelled from the family. The Maudsley Adoption Studies showed rejection to be a significant predictor of the instability of placements after one year, and in a subsequent follow-up into adolescence (Dance and Rushton, 2005).

Attachment to birth family

Rosenthal's review (1993) noted findings linking the child's attachment to his or her birth mother to disruption. Smith and Howard (Smith and Howard, 1991; Howard and Smith, 2001; Terling-Watt, 2001) also found this to be the case. The adoptions of children who were strongly attached to their birth mothers were more likely to disrupt, and problems in attachment and the parents' level of closeness to children were associated with pre-placement maltreatment or adverse conditions.

The continuing influence of birth parents has been shown to influence placement instability. Terling-Watt (2001) found this to be the most common factor, especially because adoptive kin found it difficult to set appropriate boundaries for contacts, which led to unsolicited visits, disturbance and sometimes danger to the child, and Howard and Smith (2001) noted that practitioners were concerned that appropriate boundary setting was difficult for grandparents.

Emotional and behavioural difficulties

The influence of emotional and behavioural problems on the stability of placements hardly needs to be laboured. It shows up consistently in the US (Rosenthal, 1993; Howard and Smith, 2001) and the UK literature (Rushton, 2003a). However, many studies report rather simple measures or analyses of these problems, without systematic assessments or identification of which problems carry the most risk, and which are amenable to support and therapeutic intervention. The most commonly defined problems are reviewed here.

Oppositional and conduct problems

All studies confirm the predictive power of extreme manifestations of these difficulties, such as aggression, stealing, vandalism, cruelty to others or animals and sexual acting out or abuse (Barth and Berry, 1988; Smith and Howard, 1991; Rosenthal, 1993; Berry, 1997; Quinton and Selwyn, 2005; Quinton and Selwyn, 2009).

Emotional difficulties

Emotional difficulties include depression, anxiety, fears and phobias, withdrawal and low self-image. Many studies tend to put emotional and behavioural problems together in composite EBD problem scores, but this is not a helpful approach, since there is evidence that the influence of these factors on disruption is different. Rosenthal and

Groze's survey of 779 parents (1990) suggested that it was the conduct and not the emotional problems that were predictive of disruption, a finding repeated in the Maudsley Adoption Studies (Rushton *et al*, 2001; Dance and Rushton, 2005).

Over-activity and inattention
The review by the Evan B. Donaldson Adoption Institute does not report any studies that discuss over-activity and inattention, or more formally diagnosed ADHD. This is surprising given the apparent importance of these difficulties in placement instability, their persistence through childhood and their impacts on education and peer relationships, as shown in the three studies in the UK that assessed these behaviours through systematic and validated research interviews and questionnaires (Quinton *et al*, 1998; Rushton *et al*, 2001; Dance *et al*, 2002).

Attachment
There is currently much interest in "attachment disorders" and "disturbed attachments" as sequelae of early maltreatment and as threats to placement stability (Howe, 2005; Schofield and Beek, 2006). In the English and Romanian Adoption Study, elements of a disinhibited attachment pattern were still apparent at age 11 in children adopted from Romanian institutions (Rutter *et al*, 2007). Rutter *et al* have provided an incisive discussion of attachment concepts, measures and categorisations, together with an outline of clinical implications (Rutter *et al*, 2009b). This discussion is particularly useful with respect to children with markedly adverse early experiences. In addition, a series of meta-analyses and reports from the Netherlands point to the continuation of disturbances in attachment of both the insecure and disorganised types, although most commonly for children adopted after the first year of life (van IJzendoorn, 2006).

A few studies have looked at the influence on placement stability of the development of a positive relationship between adopted children and adopters. The first Maudsley Adoption Study (Quinton *et al*, 1998) assessed the stability of placements at the end of the first year. At this point, 28 per cent were in a "less stable" category. Instability was predictable from the adopters' view at one month that forming a relationship with the child was difficult. Lack of attachment at one year was strongly related to the two principal child predictors: rejection by birth parents and overactive/restless behaviour. However, this prediction was mediated by the degree of responsive parenting, such that attachments were much more likely to develop for children with these risks when parenting was responsive early on.

There is little doubt that a list of "needs" to be addressed should include a child's attachment behaviours and 'the child's capacity to make new attachments' (Adoption and Permanence Taskforce, 2004). However, there is no professional agreement on what attachment disorders are nor whether behaviours are within a normal range or not (O'Connor and Zeanah, 2003; Barth *et al*, 2005). No reliable methods for assessing attachment prior to an adoptive placement have been found. This is to be expected since most measures of attachment require evidence from long-standing relationships. Not surprisingly, no studies have been found that have looked to see if an assessment of attachment prior to placement is able to predict attachment relationships in the new family, although it would be surprising if there were no such relationship, given the findings on the risks to placement that arise through a failure of a child to establish attached relationships with adopters. It is as yet uncertain whether such an assessment of attachment can be reliably made at this point in the adoption process.

Studies of psychosocial outcomes
There are very few studies that look prospectively at outcomes and also have sufficient detail on children's behaviours and characteristics to be useful in refining the list of needs in a way that might be helpful in matching. Prospective studies are essential to our understanding of needs and helping to decide which are likely to have most influence on the stability of placements and on outcomes. Fortunately for this review, the majority of these studies are of UK adoptions and are of recent date, although more prospective studies are beginning to

appear using data from larger samples than are usually available in the UK. For example, Simmel and her colleagues (Simmel *et al*, 2007) compared the emotional and behavioural difficulties in children from California who were adopted from foster care with adopted children who had not been fostered. Data were collected at two, four and eight years into placement via questionnaires to adopters. The children from foster care had much higher rates of disorder than the non-fostered adopted children, but both groups had many more problems than children in the general population. Difficulties were generally very persistent and the rates of disorders in the two groups tended to converge over time.

Three UK studies are outlined here: the Maudsley Adoption Studies; Selwyn and her colleagues' study of the costs and outcomes of non-infant adoptions; and the York studies of foster care. The latter, although not of adoption, have much useful information on carer and child factors associated with success or breakdown.

The Maudsley Adoption Studies

The Maudsley Adoption Studies involve two samples of permanently placed children: the first, of 61 children placed between the ages of five and nine inclusive (Quinton *et al*, 1998), and the second a sample of 133 children, of whom 101 were placed with siblings, and at least one child was between the ages of five and 11 at the time of placement (Rushton *et al*, 2001). These studies used a closely similar methodology, with interviews with adoptive parents soon after the placement and again one year later. The interviews collected both quantitative and qualitative data using "investigator based" methods (Brown, 1983), and assessed children's psychosocial adjustment according to established research criteria. Assessments of parenting used well-established interviews developed by Quinton and others (Quinton and Rutter, 1988). Measures were collected at both points in time. Similarity of methods allowed the samples to be combined for follow-up purposes.

Subsequent studies re-contacted the families when the children were between the ages of 11 and 16, on average six years after placement. At this point, 71 per cent of adoptions remained intact, although 34 per cent were showing difficulties associated with continuing behavioural problems and difficulties in the relationship between parents and children.

Predictors of both disruption and poorer outcomes in adoptions that were still intact were essentially the same as those that predicted problems at one year: the level of behavioural problems; overactivity; the failure in the development of attachments to the new family, especially the persistence of "false affection"; and also the experience of preferential rejection when still in the birth family. Failure for attachments to develop had an impact on parental sensitivity and, through that, on placement stability. By this time also, the child's age at placement, the number of prior moves and the length of time in care before placement became significant, although there is an obvious issue in that age at placement is likely to correlate with the number of moves and will determine age at follow-up. Part of the emerging effect of these variables may be due to behavioural changes associated with age and with parental age-related expectations.

The Costs and Outcomes of Non-Infant Adoptions

This study (Selwyn *et al*, 2006) was a catch-up prospective study of 130 children aged three to 11 at the time that an adoption recommendation was made in their favour in the early 1990s. Extensive information from case notes was gathered on their early lives and placement histories up to the time of that decision. These data collected from case notes included ratings of psychosocial problems at the time of placement. Ninety-six children were placed for adoption, 34 went into long-term foster placements and 16 entered unstable care careers. At follow-up, six to 11 years after the adoption recommendation, when interviews with adoptive parents were conducted, 80 (83%) of the adoptive placements were still intact. The study included a follow-up through interviews and information from social services on those children who went into care.

The main predictors of poorer psychosocial outcomes from the time of the adoption recommendation were the extent of conduct problems, overactivity and attachment difficulties. The attachment of the adopted children was somewhat better than that of the fostered group, even when attachment problems at the time of the adoption recommendation were taken into account.

The York foster care studies

These studies, using a prospective design and self-completion quest-ionnaire methodology, looked at the characteristics and fostering careers of 944 foster carers over an 18-month period (Sinclair *et al*, 2004); and a study of 596 foster placements followed up after 14 months (Sinclair *et al*, 2005b), with a further follow-up of these placements at the end of three years (Sinclair *et al*, 2005a). More successful placements were predicted for children who wanted to be in the placement; who had attractive characteristics; and who did not score highly on standard measures of disturbance and difficult behaviour at the start. A key characteristic of parents was an ability to handle disturbed attachment behaviour and to control the child without making him or her feel rejected. Over the longer follow-up, disturbed ways of relating predicted difficulties in most subsequent settings (foster care, adoption, independent living).

These studies highlighted a further feature of successful placements, and one that was almost certainly related to the child's willingness to be in placement and the development of positive relationships: "click" or "fit" – that is, that some carers and children simply took to each other. This kind of personal chemistry is not possible to predict ahead of time. For this reason, some recent practice developments in adoption have sought to capitalise on this process through "adopter-led" approaches in which an initial preference may be found by meetings, or "exchange days" at which potential adopters can learn more about individual children as a basis for expressing an interest in ones they feel attracted to (Adoption Register for England and Wales, 2010).

Data on matching

None of these prospective studies of psychosocial outcomes have presented data on matching, even on the crudest of measures such as social workers' initial views on the appropriateness of the placement. Data relevant to this may be buried in the datasets somewhere and might be worth extracting, given the paucity of information on outcomes of matching. On the other hand, the studies present a consistent picture on the child behaviours or "needs" that ought to be carefully assessed as a preliminary to matching and as a basis for discussion with adopters on issues they are likely to face and whether they feel competent to do so, as well as a basis for drawing up adoption support plans.

The needs that were the most predictive of placement success and failure were: behavioural difficulties (oppositional and conduct problems and "acting out"); overactivity and restlessness; and problems in forming attachments to new parents and families. Although these problems diminished over time for some children, they tended to be persistent and wore down adopters' and foster carers' tolerance and ability to cope. It is clear that these central issues need to be assessed as well as possible, both during the matching phase and as the placement progresses.

Summary

The idea of "meeting needs" is central to current legislation and practice guidance on adoption. Legislation sets out some broad requirements concerning the primacy of the welfare principle and the importance of a "secure environment", for which "permanence" is a prerequisite, in providing for the child's welfare. Within this, it gives preference to placements with relatives, providing that they can meet the child's needs. A further legal requirement is that due consideration is given to the child's religious persuasion, racial origin and cultural and linguistic background.

Beyond these general requirements, which effectively set a hierarchy in matching decisions, the setting out of what "needs" are to be taken into account is left to practice guidance, and this follows the areas of child development set out in the Assessment Framework.

Research that might help to identify the needs that require the most attention have predominantly come from studies of adoption disruption or termination. A number of correlates and predictors have been found: age at placement; a history of previous placement disruptions; a history of maltreatment and rejection by birth parents; and continuing attachment to and/or disturbed contact with the birth family. It seems likely that the association of these factors with placement instability and with poorer outcomes in intact placements is mediated by three important features of the child's behaviour: conduct difficulties; overactivity and restlessness (ADHD); and a failure to form attached relationships with the adoptive family.

Unfortunately, there are no data that shed any light on how well these areas of difficulty are or can be assessed prior to placement, nor on whether it is possible in advance to identify prospective adopters who might be best able to cope with them. That is, we do not know how successful the matching process is in doing this. However, it seems unlikely that the objective of matching parental capacities to children's needs can be done effectively unless matching is seen as an ongoing process requiring continuing reassessment and support after the placement.

5 Parental capacities

Research is much more abundant on the broad characteristics of adoptive parents and how these relate to the outcomes of the placements than it is on the specifics of matching. At present, the bulk of this work has been concerned with predictors of disruption, not with other aspects of outcome, and the majority of it is from the United States. This limiting of research to disruption is unfortunate since if adoptions terminate they cannot be said to have met children's needs (even if the termination seems to be better than the continuation), and, as we have seen from the previous chapter, one-quarter to one-third of adoptions may continue in a perilous condition.

In this chapter the research on parenting capacity is summarised, although few studies have given predictors of outcome from particular parenting characteristics (e.g. sensitivity, boundary setting, tolerance, resilience), or from their combination. Whether an atomistic approach to parenting skills and capacities would be helpful is unknown. Judging a range of characteristics together may be more helpful, but it would be useful to know whether differences in strengths and weaknesses – which we all have – can be summarised in a way that is helpful to matching. For example, the number of parents who are sensitive, *and* tolerant, *and* child-centred, *and* good at boundary setting, *and* resilient in the face of non-attachment may be small, but the number who are good at some of these will be much larger. Therefore, we are looking for good enough parenting capacities for a variety of children and circumstances. But to make this judgement, we need to know which capacities are essential and which can be made good enough with support and training.

Studies of outcomes

Parental characteristics

As the children for whom adoption is sought are increasingly those with "special needs", so the demographic profiles of those thought to be "suitable" as adoptive parents have become relaxed, partly because the demand for adopters outstrips the supply, but also because of challenges to the assumptions underlying previously restrictive criteria. Thus, the preference for healthy white couples of adequate income and in the age range 20–40 – favoured in an era when adoption was a way of finding children to create proxy "natural" families, and when the supply of babies was greater than the demand for adoptable children – has disappeared. Research – again, mostly on placement disruptions – has supported the widening of the criteria for eligibility, and not just because of the need to find families for special needs children. Chief amongst those factors that research has shown *not* to be risks are shown below.

Age

On the whole, increased parental age has been found to go along with *greater* stability in adoptions, not less (Groze, 1986; Barth and Berry, 1988; Berry, 1997), although differences in age are usually not marked. For example, the average difference in parental age between placements that disrupted and those that did not in Berry and Barth's 1990 report was 37 versus 44 years, suggesting that the relationship is not direct. Thus, some studies have found that older adopters are more likely to be motivated by humanitarian or religious impulses (Stolley, 1993), to have more stable relationships and more job security (Groze, 1986; Barth and Berry, 1988). Some studies have shown older parents to have more success with later adopted children than younger parents (Rosenthal *et al*, 1988; Berry, 1997;), but not all studies have found these associations (Barth and Miller, 2000). Quinton *et al* (1998) found no effects of parental age on the stability or psychosocial outcomes of 61 placements one year into placement. The age range of the mothers was 27–56 and the fathers 31–59.

It seems likely that, within broad age limits, where effects of parental age are found these effects are indexing other more powerful parental characteristics and that it is the differences in these that account for the differences in findings. The broad conclusions from these data are that the age of potential adopters is not, in itself, a risk to the stability of adoptions, although the data do not give any pointers to an upper or lower age at which risks do increase. Amongst the claimed advantage of age is that it brings more maturity. However, as Quinton *et al* (1998) have shown, maturity and parenting experience can be a disadvantage when parenting approaches that worked with the adopters' birth children do not work with the adopted ones.

Education, occupation and income
In his 1993 review, Rosenthal found four studies showing a modest association between parental education and a risk of disruption and four that did not. Four others found no association between education and risk. A similar picture emerged for income and occupational level. Some studies show no association between professional status and disruption (McRoy, 1999) and others do (Barth and Berry, 1988; Barth and Miller, 2000). If anything, the risk of disruption goes *up* as education or professional status increase. Barth and Miller's conclusion that educated parents sometimes have unreasonably high expectations of the child placed seems a plausible explanation for the associations that are sometimes found (Barth and Miller, 2000). Recent UK studies have found no associations between social status and outcomes (Quinton *et al*, 1998).

Once again, the conclusion seems to be that these factors on their own are not risks, rather that, on some occasions, they index behaviours and characteristics that are, often because of the mismatch between them and the characteristics and behaviours of the child.

Single versus two-parent adoptions
The equivocal picture continues with the issue of single versus two-parent adoptions. The majority of studies do not show any increased risk in single parent placements, despite the fact that single parents

often care for older and more troubled children, a conclusion supported by Rosenthal (1993) and McRoy (1999). Stolley has noted that single women who are willing to adopt are usually mature, tolerant and independent and often have good support networks (1993). These characteristics may account for their success with the harder to place children.

The use of single parent adoptions – virtually always women – is now very common in the US, accounting for nearly one-third of adoptions from foster care, according to the Adoption and Foster Care Reporting System (AFCARS, 2011).[13] This proportion may be even higher for adoptions by kin. Over 40 per cent of kinship adopters in Festinger's study were living alone with their adopted children (2001, 2002).

Culture and ethnicity

This important issue is dealt with separately in Chapter 6. Here, we should note that trans-ethnic placements are similar in their termination rates to those of adoptions where adopters and children have the same ethnic and cultural backgrounds.

Experience as parents

Experience as parents might be expected to be an advantage for adopters. Indeed, some authorities have argued that parents *completing* their families through adoption will be more successful than those seeking to *create* a family by it (Kadushin and Seidl, 1971; Smith and Howard, 1991). In some studies disruption rates are, indeed, lower for completers but this is not always the case. Experienced parents may be more set in their ways and less able to adapt as the adoptive relationship develops. For example, Quinton *et al* found childless couples to be more adaptable than experienced ones (1998). Once again, however, parenting experience was not a direct risk. The risk arose because of the overlap between children's characteristics and placement type, when the more problematic children were

---

13 AFCARS Report 18, Preliminary FY2010 Estimates, June 2011.

"matched" with the more experienced parents, probably under a mistaken assumption that their experience would be an advantage.

Experience as adopters or foster carers

If experience as a birth parent is an unreliable predictor of outcomes, it might be more appropriate to look at experience as adoptive parents or foster carers. There are few reports on this topic, apart from those on foster adoptions, but Barth and Berry (1988) found no association between previous adoptive experience and placement stability.

The great majority of adoptions in the US are of children currently looked after by foster carers, so there is an inevitable selection bias in these data, since foster carers are only likely to take on children with whom they have established some level of working relationship. That is, de facto "adopter-led" matching has already occurred and such adoptions might be expected to be more successful. McRoy found adoptions by foster carers to be much more stable (1999). She attributed this to their more realistic expectations of the child and greater experience in handling problems, but the above caveat still applies.

Adopter-led approaches are becoming much more common in the UK, especially through adoption exchange days, at which approved adopters can meet with children's social workers and see information, sometimes including videos, of children who are waiting for adoptive parents. These exchange days are effective in increasing placements (Adoption Register for England and Wales, 2007), but data are lacking on whether they lead to better matches. BAAF is currently undertaking a pilot project on adoption activity days, which have previously been successful in the US.

Parenting history and behaviour

It has been suggested earlier that associations between the characteristics of parents and adoption disruptions arise because the "predictive" characteristics are associated on some occasions with factors that are more directly linked to disruption. Of course, the differences in findings may also be explained by methodological differences such as sample size or representativeness, but indexing seems likely to be part of the explanation.

Parental childhood experiences

McRoy (1999) found a connection between parents' own history of abuse and the risk of abuse of an adopted or foster child. In her sample of 40 intact adoptions and 40 disrupted adoptions, 15 cases involved child abuse allegations, 13 of which disrupted. Thirty-seven per cent of the 24 adoptive parents who themselves experienced sexual, physical or domestic abuse, subsequently abused their adopted or foster children. McRoy (1999) noted that 'this group of abusive adoptive families was not well investigated prior to placement'.

An important recent addition to the understanding of the influence of parents' childhood experiences on adoption outcomes has been provided by the Attachment Representations and Adoption Study (Hodges et al, 2003).[14] This study compared parents of 63 later-placed children (age 4–8) with 48 placed in infancy over a two-year period. Parents were assessed on a variety of measures, especially the Adult Attachment Interview (AAI), which provides a classification of the extent to which adults have resolved issues around their own childhood attachment relationships (Steele et al, 1999). The children's attachment representations were also assessed using story completion approaches (Warren et al, 1996).

An AAI classification of "secure" attachment reflects an ability to tolerate and understand difficult feelings, and to deal with those of their children as well as their own. Other classifications reflect discomfort, anger or passivity in the face of negative feelings arising from their past. There were important differences between the two groups of children at placement on the extent to which their stories contained helpful and affectionate adults, and the frequency of themes involving adult punishment and stories with catastrophic endings. The later-placed children had more negative features in their stories. After two years, both groups of children made progress and the negative features in their stories diminished.

Seventy per cent of adopters were classified as secure on the AAI. This was seen as a testament to the effectiveness of assessments by

---

14 This study was undertaken by The Anna Freud Centre and Coram Family.

social services, since this proportion is higher than in the general population. Secure adult attachment representations were related to better progress in the children. Progress was much less for the children of the small group of parents with their own attachment difficulties, and these parents felt less competent and had more depression than the secure group.

The study points to the importance of taking account of parents' unresolved losses and childhood difficulties, but also of paying attention to the extent to which these have been understood and resolved. In this study, social work assessments appear to have been generally successful, although 13 per cent of approved mothers had unresolved problems. This should not rule them out, but does point to a need for ongoing and sophisticated support.

Social support

Associations have been reported between social support and placement stability (Barth and Berry, 1988; Smith and Howard, 1991; McRoy, 1999) and post-adoption family functioning (Nelson, 1985; Kagan and Reid, 1986). Conversely, low levels of support and less contact with relatives have been associated with disruption (Feigelman and Silverman, 1984; Barth and Berry, 1988). Greater stability has also been associated with contact with other adoptive parents and foster carers (Barth and Berry, 1988), and in the US, with participation in religious activities (Erich and Leung, 1998; McRoy, 1999). This association with religion is not found in studies in the UK, but religious activity may become more influential if the numbers of adopters from minority ethnic communities with strong religious involvement increases.

It is tempting to see these effects of support as a one-way street, with the implication that encouraging more family and community support will balance out the difficulties. But receiving support depends to some extent on people's ability to attract it (Quinton, 2004), with the implication that the adopters' personalities are also part of the reason for the higher disruption rates.

Nevertheless, the commitment of kith and kin to the adoption is likely to be influential. If families and friends are unsupportive of the endeavour then, at a minimum, the adopters will be denied an important day-to-day resource for parenting. Beyond this, relatives and friends may actively make life more difficult (Feigelman and Silverman, 1984). There are few UK data on this issue, but two recent studies of foster care have confirmed that kin and friends can be sources of stress as well as support and that between a quarter and two-fifths of foster carers had experienced criticism and hostility from neighbours (Farmer *et al*, 2004; Sinclair *et al*, 2004).

Expectations

A consistent theme in the research literature is the importance of adopters' expectations as an influence on outcomes. Rigid beliefs and expectations about normal child behaviour and the place of the child in the family cause difficulties. This conclusion is repeated in a large number of studies and reviews (Partridge *et al*, 1986; Rosenthal, 1993; McRoy, 1999; Pinderhughes, 1996; Berry, 1997; Barth and Miller, 2000; Evan B. Donaldson Adoption Institute, 2004). As mentioned earlier, unrealistic expectations may lie behind the associations sometimes found between adopters' education or job status and risk of breakdown (Barth and Miller, 2000).

It is important to differentiate between the origins of misplaced expectations, since the matching process can do something about some of these, but to be especially wary of others. Misplaced expectations may arise through: incorrect beliefs about child development; acceptance of social conventions; experience with children in the general population (for example, with the children of friends and neighbours); experience with parenting other children; subconscious psychological processes (e.g. "internal working models" of relationships); or from weakly or strongly held moral and religious beliefs and principles.

Expectations may become more influential the older children are at placement, since the children's own expectations of what parents do will feed into the process as well, and parents' expectations become more stretched as the parenting task increases in complexity. The interplay between expectations and age at placement may account for some of the increasing instability of placements with age. For example,

Groze (1996) found that children placed over the age of five had a more negative impact on the family. With respect to intended long-term foster placements of adolescents, Farmer *et al* (2004) have noted that, while the usual developmental task in birth families is to negotiate the relaxation of parental rules, the opposite applies in permanent placements, where new parents need to establish boundaries and gradually to tighten rather than relax them.

Stretching

The phenomenon of "stretching" refers to those placements in which parents are persuaded to take on children outside the age range with which they feel comfortable, or to take more children than they might ideally like. The term may be used to include preferences as to the child's sex as well. It is believed that stretching is a risk to the stability of placements, but no research has been found that bears specifically on this, probably because it is hard to be sure in advance what the limits of adopters' tolerance are, and hard to know in advance of placement when they have been persuaded to stretch their hopes and expectations, especially if they conceal these for fear of not being approved. Of course, stretching is also likely to involve persuading adopters to take older children, which in itself increase the risk of difficulties.

"Stretching" is also used to refer to the rigidity or flexibility of the adopters' prior conceptions of why they want to adopt a child and how they imagine the child fitting into some notion of a new or changed family. McRoy (1999) found an association between stretching in this sense and disruption. Similarly, the number of preferences expressed (Festinger, 1986) or unwillingness to take an emotionally disturbed child (Berry, 1997) both increase the risk of disruption. Ward (1997) has invoked Constantine's[15] family paradigms as a way

---

15 Constantine has characterised families as: closed families, which emphasise the family over the individual and are hierarchical in a traditional way; random families, which emphasise the needs of the individual over the group; open families, which emphasise both aspects and have consensual decision making; and synchronous families, in which members have shared values but communicate them implicitly. Somewhat unhelpfully, most families are seen to be a blend of these.

of linking patterns of expectations to the kind of family support needed.

Willingness to work with the agency

Neither expectations nor support can be managed if the adopters are not willing to work with the agency (or vice versa). Reluctance to seek information or work collaboratively were identified as indicators of the fragility of matches by both managers and practitioners in Tubbs *et al*'s (2001) unpublished report, which is summarised later in this chapter.

Agency influence on expectations

Prospective parents get their general expectations and beliefs from a wide variety of sources, and these will feed into their expectations for a particular child, but the actions of agencies are another major source of well or badly tuned parental expectations. Researchers have noted that agency factors, such as a lack of information, staff turnover, poor adoption preparation and planning for the child to join their new family are closely connected to parents' unrealistic expectations. A majority of the families (58%) in Reilly and Platz's survey (2003) said that they did not receive enough information on their child, and more than a third (37%) said the child's problems were more serious than the state agency originally told them. Poor information is a theme that recurs regularly in the UK literature (Rushton *et al*, 2001; Selwyn *et al*, 2006). It seems superfluous to add that parents are almost bound to have inadequately realistic expectations if they have no good information on which to base them.

Howard and Smith's 2001 study showed that being fully prepared for adoption is the strongest parent-related factor for predicting positive child adjustment afterwards, although, as Rosenthal noted, some parents persist with unrealistic expectations despite careful preparation (Rosenthal, 1993). For example, Schmidt *et al*'s study (1988) showed that some parents thought that their child would be less difficult to care for than the agency told them, and were confident that they could handle whatever came up. Other families reported that the placement process was too brief, preventing them and the children from getting used to each other, and forcing them together in order to meet agency and court deadlines.

Parenting style

Expectations are important, but it is the translation of expectations into behaviour that will determine the fate of placements. For this reason assessing parenting style, or the likely parenting style of couples yet to take on the task, should lie at the heart of assessments for matching. There are now an increasing number of studies that have directly assessed parenting *behaviours* and related these to outcomes, especially outcomes other than disruption. These include the Maudsley Adoption Studies;[16] a series of reports from Holland of international adoptees placed in infancy (Juffer *et al*, 2005); and the English-Romanian Adoption Study (ERA) (Rutter *et al*, 2009a).

Studies of international adoptions mostly deal with the psycho-social development of children adopted in infancy, and for this reason are not reviewed here, except to mention that there were detectable effects of maternal sensitivity on social and other areas of development at age seven (Stams *et al*, 2002). The ERA team concluded that the parenting by the adoptive families was a major influence on the children's remarkable developmental recovery, both through the parenting itself and through the parents' ability to organise services. However, variations in parenting between the adoptive families did not account for variations in the degree of psychological progress. This seemed to be more related to pre-adoptive experiences than to the family environment (Rutter *et al*, 2009a).

The Maudsley Studies assessed parenting behaviours, including expressed warmth, sensitivity and responsiveness, style of discipline, boundary setting and control, through interviews with adopters using

---

16 The two principal studies are: a) a study of 61 children placed between the ages of 5 and 9 in which the parents and one randomly selected child were assessed by interview at one and 12 months into the study (Quinton *et al*, 1998); and b) a study of sibling placements following a similar design and comparing 101 siblings and 32 singly placed children (Rushton *et al*, 2001).

well-established investigator-based interview methods (Brown, 1983; Quinton and Rutter, 1988). Adopters were interviewed shortly after the start of the placement and again at the end of the first year. Follow-up studies over longer periods made it possible to see the impact of parenting behaviours in the long run. The first study (Quinton *et al*, 1998) showed the complexity of the interaction between the children's behaviour and the style of parenting. Parenting disciplinary approaches at the beginning of the placement did not predict stability at one year. However, the two were strongly associated at the one-year point. The conclusion was that disciplinary style observed at one year was a *consequence* of the interaction between the child and the parents and reflected a downward spiral in their relationship. For this reason, matching on presumed disciplinary style would be unlikely to be helpful.

On the other hand, parental sensitivity and responsiveness did predict stability right from the start and the two remained strongly correlated with it at one year. Thus, responsiveness was a more stable parental characteristic than disciplinary style. Even so, responsiveness was affected by the child's characteristics, especially the experience of rejection by the birth family. The effect of matching of parental responsiveness to the child's behaviours and emotions was highlighted by two findings. Lower parental responsiveness carried no increased risk for children who had not been rejected or who were not overactive or restless, but was related to instability if the children had these difficulties.

Nevertheless, responsiveness was not impervious to difficulties in the children's behaviour. A six-year follow-up of a combined sample of children from this and the study of sibling placements showed that sensitive responding dropped when attached relationships were not developing. Thus, although sensitivity influenced the development of relationships and the stability of placements, it was the children's experience of rejection and the continuance of overactive and restless behaviour that drove instability in the long run (Dance and Rushton, 2005).

A practitioner study

A study by Tubbs and colleagues has reported on practitioners' views on which characteristics of adopters and adopted children are important in matching. Tubbs *et al* have reported the views of adoption administrators and practitioners on the predictors of success (2001). The administrators emphasised: the adopters' openness; their resources and compatibility with the child, including shared historical/cultural experiences; the match between the energy levels of the child and the family; and the fit between them on temperament, emotional expressiveness and expectations. The last of these involved a joint acceptance that adoption has lifelong implications, commitment to the adoption as a process, not just the act of placement, and realistic joint expectations about this process. Finally, the administrators emphasised the role of services as providers of knowledge and training and giving direct support.

Caseworkers were asked to list their predictors of success. The early indicators of success were: that the chemistry was right and a connection made with the heart; that the adoptive family was realistic about abilities and limitations; and that they could adapt their parenting style flexibly and tolerantly. Conversely, the early indicators of fragility were: a denial of difficulties and a belief that love is enough; a lack of teamwork with the agency and foster carers; rigid and intolerant parenting; and a lack of joint commitment to the process.

Matching was easier with parents who actively sought information; were willing to consider a wide range of children and to adjust their expectations accordingly; and had experience of parenting or the care of children with special needs. Conversely, matching was harder when parents downplayed special needs; discounted feedback; were too broad and vague in their adoption preferences and the implication of these for the family; and were rigid in their approach to many aspects of the adoption process.

Caseworkers were much less specific about the characteristics of the child that made matching easier. This was a rather routine list: that the child was aged under 10; had few special needs; was attractive physically and socially; and did not need a placement with siblings.

These views of administrators and caseworkers broadly agreed with the literature on special needs placements on the importance of compatibility between the children's and the adopters' expectations, their responsiveness to each other and personal and social resources. Thus, although the age, ethnic identity and personal history of the child are likely to feed into this compatibility, matching the age and ethnicity of the child to those of the prospective parents does not in and of itself ensure success or failure. It is the compatibility of parental and child expectations on these characteristics that is the key.

The child's expectation of the adoption is embedded within the child's historical experiences. What a child has come to expect from the adults providing care for him or her is the foundation of the child's behaviour. Therefore, compatibility between the expectations of the waiting child and that of the prospective parents underlies much of the discussion of demographic influences. In addition, compatibility between the expectations of the agency and prospective parents was very strongly emphasised.

Summary

What are we to make of the usefulness of the research literature to this discussion of the identification of the "parental capacities" important to the process of matching? In the first place, it is necessary to reiterate to the point of tedium, that there is no research that directly addresses the importance of matching children's needs to parenting capacities. Nevertheless, the research related to adoption outcomes and disruption does have many clear pointers to the characteristics of parents that relate to success and, therefore, to the characteristics that point to limitations or to unacceptability.

Research has cleared away many earlier preconceptions about who would and would not be suitable persons to become adoptive parents. Thus, there is little evidence that many previously emphasised demographic characteristics are bars to success as adopters or indicators of increased risk of disruption. This is true for age, single-parent status, ethnicity of adopter or child, occupation, income and educational level. Where associations have been found between these and placement difficulties, these are best interpreted as indexing proximal causes of difficulties that are sometimes but not necessarily correlated with these demographic features.

Two reviews have summarised the features of parenting style that relate to success. The Evan B. Donaldson Adoption Institute's 2004 review of adoption highlighted: commitment; a flexible and relaxed approach to parenting; realistic expectations; the adopters' ability to distance themselves from the child's behaviour; and a willingness to work with the agency and to understand that information about the child is related to success (Evan B. Donaldson Adoption Institute, 2004). Sinclair's review of foster care studies has a similar list (2005). The factors in this study were: the offer of security with persistence; the offer of tolerable closeness; sensitivity to feelings, motives for behaviour and to other attachments; the ability to set limits; and a capacity not to reinforce difficult behaviour.

Providing that expectations and beliefs can be reasonably assessed, this would at least seem to get us a long way to establishing the pool of potential adopters, and if commitment, flexibility and expectations, as measured in assessments, translated with a high degree of success into the behaviours of the adopters as parents, then we ought to be some way down the road towards increasing placement success.

It is likely that the power of even the best assessments will be nullified if children have problems that can overwhelm even the most flexible, tolerant and committed parents. Equally, these positive parental characteristics may be easier to assess with adopters who have already been or acted as parents: evidence from actual behaviour is likely to be more powerful than tests and speculations. Those who have not parented do not know which buttons will be pressed by particular actions on the part of the children. But those who have parented do not always know either, especially when the behaviours are outside or contrary to their usual experience.

Nevertheless, perhaps assessment as it is done in the best current practice may be as good as we can get, and the notion of matching parents' "capacities" to children's "needs" may be an unnecessary and utopian over-elaboration. However, there is some evidence that the fit between adopters or foster carers and children can be assessed at quite a refined level and that this can make a difference (Quinton *et al*, 1998; Kaniuk *et al*, 2004). At present, however, fit is more usually a matter of luck, as is mis-fit. Indeed, a lack of fit can arise through mistaken common-sense beliefs, for example, that experienced parents will be better than inexperienced ones at dealing with emotional and behavioural problems. It remains to be seen whether assessments can be sufficiently refined and reliable to make the finer matching of capacities and needs a reality.

6   Matching on ethnicity

In Chapter 3, the conceptual issues that are involved in matching on ethnicity and culture were outlined. As was pointed out, agencies placing children for adoption are required by law to '... give due consideration to the child's religious persuasion, racial origin and cultural and linguistic background' (Adoption and Children Act, 2002 s.1(5)), but that these considerations have to be balanced against the negative effects of delay. An argument was made for abandoning the term "race" in discussion of placements that go across different heritages, preferring the term "ethnicity" instead.

At the time of writing, the Coalition Government has issued strong directions that attempts to match on ethnicity should be set aside if they lead to excessive delay, and if prospective adopters are judged to meet "most" of the child's needs (Department for Education, 2011a). As yet, there is no advice on how to judge whether delay is excessive, nor a mechanism through which this might be adjudicated.

No research evidence has been found that might help practitioners give "due consideration" to ethnicity or decide at what point attempts at ethnic matching should be abandoned in order to prevent serious negative developmental consequences. The arguments in favour of ethnic matching commonly point to adverse effects on a child's "sense of identity" and his or her capacity to cope with racism, if a match is not achieved. If these arguments are correct, then other negative outcomes have to be serious if matching on ethnicity is to be abandoned. It seems likely that the most serious outcome of delay in finding a match will be a failure to find a stable placement at all. If this happens, then the likely consequences are, indeed, all too well documented.

As pointed out in Chapter 3, there are problems in defining a child's "ethnicity" and therefore problems in matching on it, not just because of the tendency to use broad categories such as "Asian" or "black", but also because of mistaken assumptions about the homogeneity of cultures and the problem of judging the degree of birth parents' attachment to aspects of the culture into which they were born, especially religion. In addition, the desire to match on ethnicity may conflict with a desire to keep siblings together when the siblings do not have the same birth parents.

These issues are further complicated by the high proportion of mixed-ethnicity children amongst those waiting for placement. Seventy-five per cent of minority ethnic children referred to the Adoption Register in 2010/2011 were of mixed heritage, mostly with white mothers and with fathers from minority ethnic groups. There were far more of these children registered than there were adopters with whom they might be matched, primarily because of a shortage of potential adopters for children with an African-Caribbean background (Adoption Register for England and Wales, 2005). For all these reasons, the problem of how to balance the desire to find an ethnic match against the desire to minimise delay is likely to remain a thorny one.

Arguments for matching on ethnicity

In this section, the limited research evidence on the effects of matching or not matching on ethnicity are reviewed. The first point to make, however, is that a major element in this discussion is not one that is easily resolved through research: that is, the feelings of members of all ethnicities, whether minority or otherwise, that their culture and heritage should be maintained and protected. For members of minority ethnic groups, including those in the UK, this has a long and bitter history in marginalisation and oppression and, indeed, systematic attempts to destroy their cultures, even to take their children away in order to do so.

However, in our "evidence-based" world, the arguments in favour of same-ethnicity placements usually appeal to evidence on effects or outcomes. The most commonly rehearsed arguments are: first, that trans-ethnic placements (nearly always of minority ethnic children with "white" adopters) have serious negative consequences for the development of the children's ethnic identity; and second, that same-ethnicity placements are much better at giving the child the skills and support that help them cope with racism.

As pointed out already, the classifications of ethnicity used in research and practice are extremely crude. For this reason alone, assessing the evidence in a way that might be useful to practice is very difficult. It is therefore not surprising that there are no reliable national data on how frequently matches on ethnicity are achieved, nor any agreement on what counts as a match, nor how long a match should be sought before non-matching placements are made.

It seems clear from Selwyn *et al*'s study (2010) that social workers seriously try to follow the requirement to take religion, ethnicity and language into account, but they are short on advice on how to do this and on what degree of similarity is good enough. In this study there were no placements of Asian or black children in "white" families, but about one-third of mixed ethnicity children were in such placements. Thus, 41 per cent of the children with part "black" and 19 per cent of those with part "Asian" heritages did not have this part of their heritage reflected in their placement. Conversely, only 8 per cent of the mixed ethnicity children with a part-black heritage and 18 per cent of those with a part-Asian background did not have the "white" part reflected in their match. This seemed to be more a question of the variety of available ethnic mixes amongst potential adopters than a reflection of the relaxation of matching principles.

Evidence on delays and other differences in the adoption of minority ethnic children is now becoming available. In the US, black and native-American children awaiting adoption are less likely to be placed than other ethnicities (US Government Accountability Office, 2007). Selwyn *et al*'s study referred to above (2010) provides some recent data from the UK on this issue. They found that black and Asian children were looked after for longer than both white children and those of mixed ethnicity before a permanence plan and an adoption recommendation were made. This was most strongly related to whether the family was already well known to social services rather than to ethnic issues. An adoptive placement was less likely for black and Asian children when an adoption recommendation had been made, mostly because the plan for the child changed away from adoption. This decision was almost entirely explained either by a failure to find suitable adopters or by a decision that their current non-adoptive placement was in a child's best interests. The failure to find adopters who met the social worker's specifications accounted for 30 per cent of cases where plans had changed, but it was not possible to tell whether this was because of restrictive matching criteria, insufficient efforts by social workers, or because a child was hard to place for other reasons. In multivariate analyses, the age of the child was the strongest predictor for all ethnicities of whether an adoptive placement was made.

Interestingly, social workers' views on ethnic matching may be more rigid than those of non-professionals. A study of general population attitudes on this issue suggested that people of all cultural heritages thought that the attempt to match should be abandoned if it had not been achieved after a year, although Muslim respondents were more likely to want searching for a religious match to continue for longer (Patel *et al*, 2004).

Evidence on the effects of trans-ethnic placements

In this section, the research evidence on these difficult issues is reviewed in order to see what light it can throw on them and what conclusions might be drawn on the claims and counter-claims about matching on ethnicity.

There are perennial academic debates on what may be taken to be "evidence". These murky waters will not be entered here; however, it is impossible to escape the issue of what should be taken into account in evaluating placement outcomes. For example, do the measures developed for a majority culture have the same meaning in a minority one? Are they sensitive enough to detect important differences between the outcomes for white and minority ethnic children, or are additional assessments needed? This is most obvious in the frequent failure in research on trans-ethnic placements to include measures of adopted people's experiences in relation to ethnicity and racism (Lee, 2003).

These are important considerations to bear in mind when evaluating research findings, especially when these are used to support or reject trans-ethnic placements. More straightforward limitations in research design and sampling should also be borne in mind. Two examples can be given: first, data on the effects of ethnic matching and non-matching on identity need not only to have sensitive measures, but also allow comparisons between same- and trans-ethnically placed children with similar histories and with placements in similar contexts – otherwise it will not be possible to decide whether positive or negative outcomes are a consequence of placements in general or of trans-ethnic ones in particular. Second, studies on the effects of placement type on "identity" need to compare placed children with children of the same family configuration and ethnicity in the general population, since ethnically mixed parentage itself presents offspring with a number of pressures and issues (Katz and Treacher, 2005) without adding the complications of adoption to the mix.

No studies have been found that have made the three-way comparison between children of mixed heritage: a) in the general population; b) in same-ethnicity placements; and c) in placements that cross ethnicities. Of course, the problems of defining ethnicities and assembling research samples for such a study would be formidable. These requirements for proper sampling and comparisons apply to qualitative studies just as much as they do to quantitative ones. The immediacy of personal accounts cannot overcome the consequences of inadequate research design or failure to make the necessary comparisons.

Research findings

Two arguments relating to the outcomes from trans-ethnic placements are regularly advanced: firstly, that parents of the same ethnicity are better able to help children cope with racism; and secondly, that same-ethnicity placements give children a firmer sense of ethnic identity, which in turn leads to better adjustment in adulthood. But there are also conceptual and definitional problems here. What would an acceptable cultural identity look like? Does "acceptable" mean acceptable to other members of the culture, or to the child him or herself?

It should be emphasised that the great majority of US and European research has provided data only on adoptions in infancy or very early childhood.[17] There are very few studies of placements made at the ages more common in the UK and also relatively few studies on children adopted from public care. No studies have been found of white children placed with minority ethnic parents, or of trans-ethnic placements *within* minority ethnic cultures. The evidence has also, in the past, relied heavily on US studies, mostly of the adoption of African-American children. More recently, evaluation of such place-ments has included European studies of intercountry adoptions (Lee, 2003).

It is important to note the ethnic diversity of the children placed through intercountry adoption and the differences in this from those adopted from care within the UK. In Selwyn *et al*'s study (2010), most of the minority ethnic children were of Pakistani, Bangladeshi, Indian or African-Caribbean heritage, or mixtures of these ethnicities with parents of a white European background. Studies of intercountry adoptions more usually involve children from countries as diverse as South Korea, China, Sri Lanka, Colombia, Thailand and Chile. Combining all these ethnicities as representatives of some overall class of "trans-ethnic" adoptions raises many questions. Indeed, the differences in outcome between these various ethnicities can be as informative as differences between them and same-ethnicity place-ments. Some of these differences are outlined later when issues of identity and perceptions of difference are discussed. First, the findings from the more common measures of outcome are presented.

Disruption rates
The evidence on disruption rates is reasonably consistent: there is no evidence that trans-ethnic placements are more likely to disrupt than

---

17 See Evan B. Donaldson Adoption Institute, 2008; and Lee, 2003, for a summary of samples and findings.

ones where ethnicity is matched. Indeed, some studies have shown lower disruption rates, but differences in sampling and categorisations of ethnicity are always a complication. In his 1993 review, Rosenthal found no association between placement type and disruption. Indeed, in his own 1988 study, disruption rates were lower for minority ethnic children, a finding repeated by Partridge (Partridge *et al*, 1986) and Goerge (Goerge *et al*, 1995). The major study in the UK by Thoburn and her colleagues (2000) also found no difference in disruption rates between same- and trans-ethnic placements. Studies on intercountry adoption often fail to give disruption rates, possibly because these rates are very low but probably because the adoptions are mostly made in infancy (Palacios *et al*, 2005). The occasional earlier US study of within-country adoptions does point to higher disruption rates (Berry, 1997), but it seems safe to conclude that there is no difference between same- and trans-ethnic placements as far as disruption rates are concerned.

Psychosocial outcomes
Of course, just because a placement remains intact does not mean that there are no negative psychosocial outcomes. However, differences on standard measures of psychosocial functioning, such as emotional and behavioural disorders or self-esteem, have seldom been found when same-ethnicity placements are compared with placements of minority ethnic children adopted into "white" families (McRoy *et al*, 1984; Shireman *et al*, 1987; Feigelman, 2000; Thoburn *et al*, 2000). Similarly, few differences have been found in adjustment to family, school and the community. Levels of self-esteem are usually about the same, a finding confirmed by Juffer and van IJzendoorn's meta-analysis (2007). The quality of parenting appears to be the principal influence on these outcomes in both same-ethnicity and trans-ethnicity placements (Stams *et al*, 2002; van IJzendoorn, 2006).

An exception to the usual finding of "no differences" is the study by Howard and Smith (2001, 2003) in which black children in "transracial" adoptions had more behaviour problems than children in "same-race" adoptions, although there were not significant differences on measures of satisfaction, closeness, or the impact of the adoption on the family. These children were placed on average at 6.8 years from backgrounds that included serious neglect, abuse, alcohol and drug exposure and multiple foster placements. This later age at placement sets this study apart from most other investigations of trans-ethnic adoptions.

The Howard and Smith study raises a further issue when judging the relevance of a great many of these comparisons for matching children from care in the UK. That issue is the much earlier age at adoption of these samples compared with the majority of within-UK adoptions. This issue can affect many comparisons made *within* studies as well, for example, black adopted children both in same-ethnicity and trans-ethnicity placements sometimes show higher levels of emotional and behavioural disturbance than placements of other ethnicities. However, black children are often placed later, and age at placement and its correlated major adversities prior to adoption are major predictors of higher rates of difficulties[18] (Weinberg *et al*, 2005).

Identity

As pointed out above, predictions about the effects of trans-ethnic placements on personal and cultural identity are part of the argument against placements of this kind, but there are a great many gaps and methodological shortcomings in the available research when trying to decide how big a problem this is. Lee has pointed out the paucity of reliable and valid measures of "racial/ethnic identities" in the studies (2003). Comparisons are often made under the assumption that the ethnic aspects of the placement are a top-level influence on a variety of outcomes, without trying to take into account a range of possible other explanatory variables such as age at placement, prior experiences, country of origin and adoptive family functioning.

In addition, insufficient emphasis has been given to identity as a developmental process, with the danger of drawing general con-

---

18 See also the review of research relevant to children's needs in Chapter 4.

clusions from effects that may be age-related, for example, the early years at school are a time when social comparisons develop, with a focus on personal traits and characteristics (Damon and Hart, 1988). Measures taken at this time are likely to reflect such processes. This may be why identification with the adoptive parent's culture is sometimes reported as strong at that time, with some confusion in adolescence and a more secure relationship to ethnicity in adulthood, as found in Freundlich and Lieberthal's descriptive study of South Korean adopted people (2000).

Research on identity has mostly looked at the dissatisfaction or unhappiness of adopted young people with their appearance and skin colour, or at their comfort with or separation from a minority ethnic heritage. Personal accounts of the experience of trans-ethnic adoption are very powerful, but also reflect the diversity of responses to this experience (Harris, 2006).

The findings on identity are superficially similar to those on other psychosocial outcomes but also point to a greater complexity. The major prospective US studies that have compared minority ethnic children in same and trans-ethnic placements showed no differences in self-concept scores or overall adjustment to school, peers, family and community (Evan B. Donaldson Adoption Institute, 2008).

However, differences have been found on whether children were proud of their ethnic heritage and identified with it, or not. Broadly speaking, the findings suggest that trans-ethnically placed children remain generally proud of their heritage but are less likely to identify themselves as part of that culture (Silverman, 1993). McRoy and colleagues' (1984) study found that only 30 per cent of trans-ethnically placed children identified themselves as "black", preferring terms like "mixed" or "human race", and in Vroegh's study (1991), 83 per cent of 17-year-olds in same-ethnicity adoptions identified themselves as "black" compared with only 33 per cent of those who were trans-ethnically placed.

These findings are consistent with other earlier US studies that show that trans-ethnically adopted children can feel more identified with the white culture than those in same-ethnicity placements

(Hollingsworth, 1997), but other major studies reveal the complexities in interpreting these outcomes. For example, Brooks and Barth (1999) found secure racial/ethnic identities in adulthood for both Asian and African-American trans-ethnic adopted people. Nevertheless, about half of them reported unease about their appearance. Unfortunately, a comparison with young people of the same ethnicity in the general population on discomfort with the racial/ethnic aspects of their appearance was not available.

Juffer's study of seven-year-old intercountry adopted children also showed differences in concerns about appearance and identification according to their country of origin. For example, 59 per cent of children from Sri Lanka, 32 per cent from Colombia and 23 per cent from South Korea had said they wanted to be white. This wish not to appear different went along with mothers' and teachers' reports of behaviour problems for the Sri Lankan and Colombian children (Juffer, 2006).

Coping with difference

Studies of the effects of trans-ethnic adoption on identity often reflect a somewhat static conceptualisation of identity, but the studies do sometimes reflect another important issue for adopted people: coping with difference. This is not a new issue: indeed, it was first raised in Kirk's seminal work, *Shared Fate* (1964), in which he argued for a link between the adopters' and the adopted people's acknowledgement of loss and of the real differences between adoptive and birth families, and the relationship of this to mental health.

Of course, this problem is present in all adoptions, but children of one ethnicity adopted into a family with a different one face additional differences with which they have to come to terms. These differences involve not only appearance but often differences in culture and place of birth as well. So coping with difference lies somewhere between the personal tasks of identity formation and the social tasks of coping with racism.

To date, there is little research that focuses on coping with difference. Alstein and Simon (1991) report that about one-third of trans-ethnically placed children in their study reported problems because they looked different from their parents, and Juffer's (2006) study of seven-year-olds also found intercountry adopted children to have problems because of this, with difficulties being more marked for children whose skin tone differed the most from that of the adopters and of those in their immediate social surroundings. Discomfort with the feeling of difference seems more connected to the surrounding social environment than to difference from the adoptive parents and their birth children. Brooks and Barth's (1999) study showed persisting levels of discomfort with difference in the absence of problems in ethnic identification. The sense of difference can also apply to feelings about the adopted people's own ethnic culture, so that there may be a sense of distance from both the adoptive culture and the culture of identification.

Coping with racism

The ability of same-ethnicity adopters to help a child cope with racism is one of the two main arguments in favour of same-ethnicity placements. There is no doubt that minority ethnic children can experience a great deal of racist abuse, bullying and social isolation. Adoption may give additional impetus to this, but it is not known whether trans-ethnically placed children experience more racism than those in same-ethnicity placements. In the UK, Thoburn and her colleagues (2000) spoke to 24 adopted people between the ages of 11 and 30. Children in same-ethnicity placements were confident about dealing with racism and described how their parents helped them with this. They also thought that living in an ethnically mixed area was of help. Children placed with white families were also positive about the help they got in tackling racism, but also emphasised the value of linking up with other black youngsters.

There are many vivid accounts of all these issues in the lives of trans-ethnically placed individuals in Perlita Harris's collection of adopted adults' accounts of their experiences (2006).

Family and social influences

Given the apparent strength of the argument about helping a child to cope with racism, it is surprising how little direct evidence there is on this issue. The key question here is not whether the personal experiences of adopters from minority ethnic cultures enable them more easily to help a child – there is no reason to suppose that this experience does not give them an advantage – but whether adopters of a different ethnicity can find ways of making up for this lack of experience. That is, does an ethnicity similar to that of the child give same-ethnicity adopters a decisive advantage, or can this be made up for in other ways?

It seems plausible that living in an area of mixed ethnicity will help normalise the experience of trans-ethnic adopted children, but there is very little direct research on this topic. The young people interviewed in Thoburn *et al*'s study (2000) emphasised the importance of peer relationships in helping them cope. Other studies have shown that the sense of physical difference can be greater for those growing up in predominantly white neighbourhoods (Feigelman, 2000). However, it is unlikely that the demography of a neighbourhood will be sufficient to make up for any shortcomings that might arise because of ethnic differences between adopters and adopted children. Direct family contacts with adults with an ethnicity similar to that of the child are probably important, but at present this is an un-researched area.

It seems clear that the quality of parenting is the most powerful influence on a broad range of psychosocial outcomes. This is so well established for normal development in birth families within and across cultures that the point does not need to be laboured or bolstered by references. The main features of effective parenting were set out in Chapter 5. But the question remains whether parents in trans-ethnic placements can facilitate the normal development of a sense of identity and efficacy in their children, and what in addition might help in this.

Writers in the US have set out a number of different stances that adopters in trans-ethnic placements take. As yet there is little research on this, but a conceptual framework is emerging (Frasch and Brooks, 2003). Lee has described four parental stances (Lee, 2003). The first, *cultural assimilation*, involves parents taking a "no difference" or "colour blind" approach, which effectively leads to the transmission of the parents' majority ethnic values. The second stance, *enculturation*, acknowledges differences and encourages the child's knowledge of his/her culture, and provides opportunities for learning about it. Paradoxically, this may pull against the child's need to come to terms with the parents' culture as well. The third stance, confusingly called *racial inculcation*, focuses on the skills necessary for coping with racism, but places less emphasis on ethnic identity. The fourth stance is one of *child choice*, in which parents try to provide the child with experiences and opportunities and adjust their own socialisation efforts in line with the child's interests and wishes.

Evidence on the frequency with which these different approaches are used and on their relative effectiveness is very sparse. The first approach may be the most problematic because it can be the most rigid. However, the four approaches are not mutually exclusive, and caring and flexible parents are likely to try a variety of methods when dealing with problems and issues as their children grow up.

The Minnesota Transracial Adoption Project used a prospective follow-up design to look at the orientation of black transracial adopted adolescents towards their own Africentric reference group and their parents' Eurocentric reference group. This "ecological competence" was reflected in their awareness and understanding of issues and differences around ethnicity, and their use of appropriate strategies in different ethnic contexts (DeBerry *et al*, 1996). The researchers then looked to see whether ecological competence was influenced by "family racial socialisation", categorised as either de-emphasis or denial of difference; a bicultural approach; or a multiracial one.

The majority of parents were "bicultural" early in the placement; that is, they tried to promote the values of both cultures. But by the time the children reached adolescence, as reported both by themselves and the adopters, they were either in the de-emphasis/denial or the ambivalent groups, and tended to emphasise Eurocentric cultural values. This did not affect the adolescents' overall adjustment but did go along with a weaker orientation towards an African-American reference group, compared with non-adopted black adolescents.

Along with this, psychological disturbance worsened in adolescence. This was accounted for overall by the socialisation pattern plus the reference group orientation scores taken together, but there were no straightforward paths between these. That is, it was not possible to decide whether the socialisation pattern drove the reference group orientation and through this led to greater psychological disturbance. Adolescence is often associated with raised levels of psychosocial disturbance for same-ethnicity adopted children (Maughan and Pickles, 1990; Fergusson *et al*, 1995), which often declines as the children get older, but it is not known whether this was true for the Minnesota Study.

So far, this area lacks telling and decisive research findings that would allow firm conclusions on whether trans-ethnic placements markedly affect the development of children's understanding of and comfort with their ethnic heritages, and whether disturbances in this lead to psychosocial maladjustment of one kind or another. Several studies point to an association between poorer resolution of identity and identification issues and more psychosocial difficulties or unhappiness. For example, Cederblad *et al* (1999) found that for internationally adopted individuals in Sweden, perceived discrimination and ambivalence about ethnic identity was associated with emotional distress, behavioural problems and lower self-esteem, even when family structure and relationships were taken into account. Conversely, the South Korean adopted adolescents in the US studied by Yoon (2001) had better adjustment and higher self-esteem when the parents supported exploration of their ethnic background and when parent–child relationships were good.

Findings such as these are important, but many questions remain. Is there a consistent direction to these effects (e.g. does more identity confusion lead to other psychosocial problems, or vice versa), or are both outcomes manifestations of the same underlying unease? That is, are unhappiness, misbehaviour and confusion over "who I am" part of a more general distress that attracts to itself various felt dissatisfactions with aspects of the adopted person's life? If lack of "genealogical connectedness" (Owusu-Bempah, 2006) is the prime driver of other problems, then attending to that confusion is a key to meeting many psychological needs that will otherwise remain unresolved, and same-ethnicity placements may have a distinct advantage. If the picture is more complex and diffuse, then issues of connectedness are amongst the issues to be addressed, but not a key to other problems.

Summary

Matching parents and children on ethnicity is now encouraged in law and firmly established as a principle in practice. Arguments in favour of matching cannot be resolved by evidence on the effects of matching or non-matching alone because the issue also involves strong feelings concerning the rights of cultures to maintain themselves, to whom children belong culturally, and who should care for them (Massiah, 2005).

Despite this, arguments in favour of ethnic matching usually cite the psychosocial benefits arising from it and the ill effects of not matching. Research, mostly from the US, has not provided clear and decisive evidence to support this point of view. Disruption rates for matched and not-matched children are much the same and there are few differences in most psychosocial outcomes, including self-esteem. On the other hand, trans-ethnically placed children are less likely to identify with being "black", even though they generally are proud of their ethnic heritage. No studies have been found that have looked in more detail at their identification with particular features of a culture, nor at the strength of a child's attachment to their birth parents' religion.

Research evidence is also equivocal with regard to the enhanced ability of same-ethnicity placements to help a child cope with racism, which such placements are strongly believed to provide, although it does suggest that the sensitivity of non-matched adopters to problems with racism is an important element. Developing the ability to cope with racism is one of the most strongly advanced arguments against trans-ethnic placements but is much under-researched, as is the extent to which minority ethnic members of the local community can provide the support and information that trans-ethnically placed children need. Some studies of birth families do point to the value of this and to the attempts of "white" parents to provide this kind of environment (Harman and Barn, 2005). We do not know of any studies that look at whether "white" adopters of trans-ethnically placed children successfully facilitate links with aspects of the child's heritage in this way.

Objecters to research that shows little difference in placement outcomes commonly argue that the wrong things are being assessed or that measures are not sensitive enough to detect important differences. There is some force to this argument but, perhaps because of the sensitivity of the topic, commentators can be more severe on the methodological limitations of individual studies that do not support their preferences than on those that do. Also, within this debate, insufficient attention is given to children's and young people's own agency in constructing their identities (Tizard and Phoenix, 2002) and, perhaps, too many assumptions are made about what their identity *ought* to be, especially with respect to their ethnic heritage.[19]

This issue is particularly salient for those with a mixed heritage. It may be the lack of evidence that led Rushton and Minnis, in their careful review of the topic, to conclude that ethnic matching was preferable, despite the fact that they drew the same conclusions from the available data as does this review (Rushton and Minnis, 1997).

The formidable difficulties of definition, design and measurement when researching the effects of placements within and across ethnicities have been stressed. At present, comparisons tend to be rather crudely between same- versus trans-ethnic placements, or very broadly defined ethnic groups, for example, "Hispanics" versus "African Americans" in the US literature. Many key comparisons remain to be made, especially for children of mixed heritage, where too much emphasis may currently be given to the "one drop of blood" principle (Owusu-Bempah, 2005), and too little attention paid to the

---

19 For a personal discussion of the meaning of "identity" outside the field of adoption, see Maalouf, 2003.

"white" part of the child's heritage (Barn, 1999). There is, for example, the need for a three-way comparison on identity and on coping with racism between children of mixed heritage in the general population, in same-ethnicity placements and in placements that cross ethnicities.

Finally, the purpose of this report should be stressed – that it is a conceptual and research review of matching in adoption. It should be clear that the conceptual, definitional and emotional difficulties surrounding matching or not matching on ethnicity have received as much attention as that given to research studies on effects and out-comes. This is inevitable, given the sensitivity of the topic. Never-theless, there is little research to offer guidance to the practising social worker on what might reasonably be taken to constitute a match, on how to take into account the personal as well as the generic aspects of heritage, including, for example, the strength of the birth parents' religious beliefs and observance, or on when the search for a match should be abandoned in favour of a hoped-for permanent trans-ethnic placement, and on what the outcomes from this decision might be, compared with matched placements.

7 Assessment and research 1: children

The preceding review of research dealt with a great number of studies that address key questions important to decisions on matching, but also made clear that there are many gaps and inconsistencies in the findings so far. This complicates the relationship of research to practice, even before the problems of translating research findings into practical advice are considered. As pointed out at the beginning of this review, there are remarkably few studies that directly address the process of matching and evaluate its outcomes. There may be unpublished research on this topic conducted by agencies for their own purpose, but this is likely to suffer from problems of sampling and data consistency.

This review is confined to published research that sets out its methods and findings clearly. It focuses on what research can say about the assessment of the children's needs and parents' capacities that are most strongly related to placement success. There is a shortage of prospective studies on placement outcomes, but those that have been done show that the predictors of poorer outcomes in intact placements are the same as those that predict disruption, so much of relevance to matching can be drawn from the disruption literature.

The lack of a substantial body of prospective studies on matching is a severe limitation as, indeed, is the lack of systematic accounts of how assessments of children and adopters are brought together in the matching process. It might be said that research ceases to be helpful to practice at this point because decisions are case-specific, so that averaged associations across populations and samples are no longer helpful to decision-making.

This assumption is wrong for a number of reasons: first, many, if not most, of the characteristics of the children and prospective adopters that practice advice emphasises in assessment and matching derive from the findings of research, i.e. emotional and behavioural problems, attachment difficulties, resilience, parental warmth, boundary setting and facilitation, to name but a few. Second, research has shown that features that were thought to be risks are not. These include parental age, marital status, family structure or lack of parenting experience, as well as a child's emotional problems, as distinct from their behavioural difficulties. Research has also highlighted things that have been insufficiently attended to in assessment and support, such as the persistence of overactive and restless behaviour.

This review does not set out to provide an account of the assessment process or to be a survey of agency practice, although the important study by Dance and her colleagues (2010) is referred to frequently in this chapter. However, it is necessary to give a brief overview of the assessment process in order to relate the information social workers are advised or required to gather to the findings from research.

For both children's needs and parenting capacities, the questions of the *hierarchy* and *specificity* of needs assessments have to be considered. By "hierarchy" is meant whether some features relevant to matching, such as ethnicity, are given priority over others. "Specificity" refers to the degree of detail needed in assessments made prior to placement. For example, is it good enough to note "emotional and behavioural problems", or do we need to differentiate prior to placement between, say, inattention and restlessness, oppositional and conduct problems, and attachment difficulties? If so, how much expert knowledge and training is required to assess these with a degree of accuracy required for matching? This question of specificity has considerable implications for social work training and education.

In this chapter, the advice on what to assess and how to do this with children and prospective adopters and the relationship of this advice to research will be discussed. But first, the positioning of assessment in the process of adoption is outlined, in order to provide the context for the collection of information relevant to matching. There is a useful summary of this process and variations in it across agencies in Dance *et al*'s study (2010).

Assessing children's needs

Local authorities have a statutory requirement to set out a plan for permanence for any child for whom a court makes a care order, and to evidence how this plan might be fulfilled. The plan may include a return home, long-term foster care, special guardianship or adoption (HM Government, 2010).

A plan for adoption must be approved by an adoption panel, which is a statutory panel of experts and lay persons fulfilling the requirements of the Adoption Agencies Regulations 2005. Evidence compiled by social services departments is presented to this panel in the form of written reports, and the panel makes a recommendation to an adoption agency on: a) whether the plan for adoption should be approved and a placement order applied for; b) separately, whether persons applying to be adopters should be approved and, if appropriate, the profile of the children for whom they are thought to be suitable; and c) whether a particular match should be pursued.

The decision to recommend a child for adoption is taken by the social services department that holds case responsibility for them. This decision is generally made as part of a review of plans for the child. If the plan is for adoption, the assessments that support the recommendation are compiled, most usually by the children's social worker, often with advice and guidance from a specialist in adoption work. Thirty per cent of authorities in Dance *et al*'s study (2010) transferred case responsibility to a specialist team, usually after a placement or care order had been made.

The assessment of the child must be conducted by someone who is "Act qualified"; that is, someone with at least three years' post-qualifying experience in adoption or childcare, or is supervised by someone who meets these criteria. The recommendation to the panel is presented through the Child Permanence Report (CPR) (formerly the BAAF Form E), in line with the Adoption Agencies Regulations 2005. The BAAF template for the CPR was used in 88 per cent of agencies surveyed by Dance *et al* (2010). In this study, there was no involvement of the adoption/permanence team in completing the CPR in 84 per cent of the authorities, but 59 per cent had arrangements for social workers to consult child psychology specialists or had such professionals attached to their adoption teams.

The CPR is used to present the case for adoption to the panel, and is also the source of important information for the Adoption Register, and a record that adopted people may later access to help them understand the reasons for their adoption. Finally, the birth parents have an opportunity to comment on the CPR and what is recorded there. These additional uses of the report require a certain finesse on the part of social workers in providing accurate assessments whilst minimising distress to birth parents and later to adopted adults.

The structure and content of the CPR

The CPR is split into: a) the information that social services are required to provide (Parts A1 to A5); and b) other required inform-ation if it is relevant, such as details on relatives or other people with parental responsibility for the child (parts B, C and D); plus the wishes and feelings of the child and the birth parents, if this information can be collected, e.g. if the child is not too young and/or the whereabouts of the birth parents are known.

Part A1 presents information on the child's characteristics, ethnic and religious background, family history and chronology of care since birth, current circumstances and psychosocial development, including medical reports, education and statementing. It is this section, there-fore, that is most relevant to matching and which will be discussed here. The medical and educational report may contain "top level" hierarchical needs, for example, on learning difficulties or disabilities.

These data are followed by a descriptive and evaluative report, which contains the important information necessary to begin to match the child's emotional and behavioural development to adopters with the capacity to manage and ameliorate needs the child may have. This section includes: a physical description of the child, especially any impairment; his or her personality; interests, likes and dislikes; health (including a summary from the agency medical adviser); education (including the Personal Education Plan); identity; self-care skills; and social presentation. Emotional and behavioural development and family and social relationships are subsumed under the heading of 'Child's history since birth'. The data recorded in this section cover the seven areas in the "child side" of the assessment triangle as set out in the Assessment Framework (Department of Health *et al*, 2000). Advice on what should be taken into account is given in brief notes at the end of the form, to which the social worker is directed through numbers that identify the relevant notes.

All of the evaluative sections rely on the ability of the person compiling the report to synthesise and balance the information that they have recorded and summarised. The sections also rely on a social worker's knowledge and training in assessing emotional and behavioural development and attachment, and their judgement on when to call for specialist opinions. The assessments also require careful observation of the child and the current carers, as well as information from the carers themselves. The notes remind the social worker of key aspects of socio-emotional development, which have hopefully been covered in their training.

The reminders cover the following areas.

The child's history since birth (emotions, behaviour, attachment)

The reminders in this section ask for information on: birth family structure; the child's relationship with their birth and extended family; the child's experience of being cared for by others; experiences of abuse and how this has affected their emotional and behavioural development; and their current level of emotional, behavioural and social development, with a special focus on their capacity for making and sustaining relationships, for which additional notes are provided. For example:

- *How do people who care for them describe them in terms of warmth, enjoyment or wariness of intimacy, their playfulness, their responses to daily routines, to boundaries being set and to change in routines or circumstances?*
- *How do the principal carers observe the child's developing relationships with those outside the family such as friends, children at school,*

teachers? Do they maintain appropriate wariness of strangers, or are they over-familiar?

There is no explicit reminder to assess conduct, emotional problems or overactivity and restlessness systematically, even though these are also predictors of placement stability.

Identity

The reminders on identity cover physical capacities, ethnic identity (sic), language, religion, sex and sexuality. The reminders on identity point out that:

Each child will have a developing sense of who they are and what is important in the world around them. This will become the basis of self-esteem and identity. There are a number of factors that build towards self-esteem and identity.

And that:

Each of these factors singly and in combination will influence the way the child not only feels and thinks but also behaves and makes relationships. It will be central to their sense of belonging in respect of important people and their sense of community, culture and wider society. The people who care for them and provide them with opportunities and guidance will be vital in this. Adoption will have an important impact upon the child's developing sense of self, including the acquisition of an "adoption identity".

Self-care skills and social presentation

The CPR also includes notes on self-care skills and social presentation, which are part of the "child side" of the assessment triangle. These include evaluations of the child's age-appropriate and physical capacity to care for her/himself, and suggest that the assessment describes:

. . . the child's daily routines including eating, hygiene, getting dressed, bedtimes, leaving for playgroup/nursery/school . . . any

specific factors that need to be taken into account in placing the child in an adoptive family? This should include any special arrangements needed to support the child in developing their self-care skills or daily routines.

The notes on all these areas are hard to disagree with. However, they do list characteristics that are influential in a child's construction of who he or she is, but some more so than others, depending on age. For these reasons, a social worker is often asked to predict what is likely to be important in the future, often some time into the future, and to plan for what the child might then want to know about the past and to incorporate into her or his sense of self.

Assessment and measurement issues

It is clear from the above information that the ways in which assessments of the key drivers of placement success or instability, e.g. behavioural problems, overactivity and restlessness, and difficulties in making relationships ("attachment" in a broad sense) are to be made is left to the experience and "practice wisdom" of those making the assessments, and their judgement on when to call for expert opinion. An experienced worker will read the case files, talk to those who have worked with the family, talk to the current carers and call on specialist advice, but systematic assessments on psychosocial development around the key predictors of adoption success are usually based on descriptive information that is often not criterion-based.

Does this matter? A good practitioner or clinician will come to a balanced view on the specific issues for the individual he or she is trying to help. The assessment of the needs of children as set out above requires a thorough training in child development, and an ability to assess these features, to see them in the round and put them in context. This view will be based on training and experience, sometimes backed up with specific tests for particular problems, for example, to assess the degree and specificity of learning difficulties.

This reliance on professional judgement appears to be the view taken in Munro's reports on child protection (2010, 2011). Of course, this reliance depends crucially on the quality and relevance of social work training in child development and child placement practice, as well as on the availability of psychological and other expertise. It is not certain that we are anywhere near that desirable state of affairs.

In addition, assessments of children for whom adoption is the plan have a number of extra complications. First, the majority of children currently being placed are very young.[20] This is a desirable state of affairs but makes assessment of the key drivers of adoption success very difficult: consider the problems of applying the advice on assessing emotions, behaviour, attachment, identity and self-care skills. Second, assessments are being made at a time of instability in the child's life when she or he is being looked after and when the carers and social workers may be strangers to him or her. Third, these assessments will be crucial in choosing families who will hopefully be able to address the child's needs. Finally, adoption is such a radical step that comparable data on what predicts success and failure are very important for both policy and practice. If comparable data are desirable, then consistency in what is meant by particular difficulties is necessary. In short, this requires criteria and, hopefully, acceptable measurement. Without this, regular evaluation of the factors and processors underlying successful and unsuccessful matching and understanding differences between agencies in these outcomes will be very difficult.

Assessment and measurement tools

The Dance *et al* study (2010) asked agencies about their use of tools to help in assessments. Sixty-four per cent reported using "sibling checklists" and other tools developed by BAAF, but the authors of the report considered that use of these kinds of instruments were even more common. Checklists are generally aide-memoires for practitioners, the aim of which is to make sure that important topics and questions are covered. They have some potential as measurement

---

20 BAAF's summary of official adoption statistics for the year ending 31 March 2010 reports the age at adoptions from care as: under 1 = 2%; 1–4 years = 70%; 5–9 years = 24% (www.baaf.org.uk/res/statengland).

tools, but at present are not set up to do this. Attachment problems were often assessed by psychologists or through specialist attachment projects, but it was not known whether these were applying a common framework amenable to some kind of consistent recording of the assessments.

The Integrated Children's System (ICS) is a series of forms that accompany the requirements and timetables for the care of children in need and looked after children. The forms are set out as adaptable "exemplars" that are intended to collect information on the progress and development of a child and on the decisions made about his or her future at specified points during the child's "journey through care". The assessment of the child and the family are based on the assessment triangle.

At the time of writing, the future of this system is in doubt and major revisions, or indeed its abandonment, are likely, but the Assessment Framework (Department of Health, 2000) remains a key underpinning of assessments. The major critique of the implement-ation of this system has been its bureaucratic nature, both in timing and content, and the reliance on data collection through tick-boxes, the so-called "tick-box culture".

This criticism has some force, but it should be seen as a critique of the implementation of the system rather than of its philosophy. The tick-boxes were intended to *alert* the assessor to strengths and problems in each area, rather than to be rigid or prescriptive. Completing the forms was not intended to be a mechanical process – the questions are a guide to assessors, who then have the responsibility of analysing and synthesising the information. Completion of the assessments is meant to be a collaborative exercise with families and others who may have important information (Cleaver *et al*, 2004). It should also be remembered that this system came into being because of serious concerns about the quality of care planning and the monitoring of children's developmental progress.

Assessors were also recommended to use other standardised instruments such as the Strengths and Difficulties Questionnaire

(Goodman, 1999) or the HOME Inventory as additional aids to the gathering of information. The HOME Inventory (Caldwell and Bradley, 2001) comprises four age-graded modules designed to record, from the social worker's observations, the quality and quantity of stimulation and support available to a child in the home environment. The Dance *et al* study (2010) shows that agencies use some of these instruments when compiling the CPR. However, since they are not used systematically or on every child, they do not form a set of data suitable for use or analysis beyond the case level.

The CPR was to be integrated with the ICS. As outlined above, the CPR is the main assessment instrument relevant to matching. A further set of forms devised for the ICS – the Assessment and Progress Records – were designed to track the progress of children who stayed within the care system for some time. These, like the core assessment in the ICS, provide age-related exemplars covering: pre-birth to 12 months; 1–2 years; 3–4 years; 5–10 years; 11–15; and 16 years and over. These forms provide systematic coverage of the areas of psychosocial development contained within the CPR, including emotional and behavioural problems, identity and attachment, together with criterion-based rating scales.[21]

To date, these records have been little used, but have potential as an addition to the toolkit that might be helpful to practitioners, with the additional advantage of tracking the progress of children who do and do not enter adoptive placements. Systematic assessment of this nature might be valuable not only in the process of assessment and matching, but also in research understanding its outcomes. However, without training and essential background knowledge on parenting and child development, *any* forms can come to be seen as a bureaucratic chore and their value in promoting good assessments and inter-agency working lost (Cleaver and Walker, 2004a, 2004b).

---

21 The author must admit to a substantial involvement in the development of these records.

The reliability of assessments of children's needs

No reports have been found on the quality and reliability of assessments of children's needs and development. However, recent data from the Adoption Register for England and Wales suggest that the situation is far from satisfactory. The Register has kindly provided information on whether children referred to it are said to have emotional, behavioural or attachment problems.[22] It will be remembered that these are major predictors of placement problems and disruption.

The Register data on these difficulties can be compared with the Office for National Statistics (ONS) epidemiological surveys of looked after children and of children in the general population (Meltzer *et al*, 2000, 2003). The comparison is restricted to children aged five and over because the ONS survey did not include younger children. Since the Register is often trying to find placements for children who are harder to place, we might expect the rates of psychosocial difficulties to be high, even though the Register returns are unlikely to have followed the stringent diagnostic criteria used in the ONS reports. The Register returns for 2010/2011 report 26 per cent of children as having "behavioural difficulties", compared with 36 per cent of looked after children in the ONS survey, and 10 per cent of Register children were said to have severe emotional difficulties compared with 11 per cent of the ONS children.

The Register does not have a category for attention deficit disorders – the most persistent of difficulties – and the ONS survey did not assess attachment problems because of the difficulty in doing so in this population of children. The number of Register children recorded as having attachment problems – 17 per cent – seems low, given the ages and likely attachment experiences of children included in the comparison. This figure also seems somewhat low given the current attention paid to attachment concepts in practice and the practice literature.

---

22 We are grateful to Andy Stott, Adoption Register Manager, for providing these data.

Comments on the assessment of children's needs

The driving principle behind adoption is to meet the developmental needs of children that would otherwise not be met if they remained where they are. This is true of intercountry adoptions and adoptions of children from the care system.

Research studies on adoption outcomes and disruptions have consistently shown those characteristics and behaviours of these children that are most strongly predictive of placement difficulties. Age at placement is one of the strongest of these but this is substantially because of its association with emotional and behavioural problems, notably difficulties in making and sustaining relationships ("attachment problems"), oppositional and conduct problems and overactive and restless behaviour ("ADHD").

A number of other major "needs" share centre stage at present. These are the needs related to the development of "identity" and "self-esteem", notions that are often vaguely defined but powerful in their appeal. Matching on ethnicity and on the maintenance of contact with the birth family are especially linked to the hypothesised consequences for identity development if they are not adequately addressed in matching. Both of these "needs" are argued for on the basis of rights as well as effects, although arguments on effects are commonly used to support the importance of taking these needs into account when matching.

This is not an argument to support the down-playing of these two elements in matching, but questions do arise as to the emphasis given to them compared with the effort made in assessing other developmental needs, especially those around emotional and behavioural development. Attachment issues appear prominently in the practice literature, but the assessment of attachment difficulties, or potential attachment difficulties, depends on sophisticated training. This does not appear to be common in practice.

Of course, the assessment of these developmental needs, as well as those related to educational progress and attainment, is difficult with young children, especially when the circumstances under which the assessment is made are often unstable. For this reason, judgements based on the hypothesised consequences of the child's prior experiences, as well as on the capacities of adopters to deal with these, necessarily come into play. In both cases, much of the judgement on needs will be based on clinical/practice hunches and experience. The conclusion from this is that the assessment of many needs will remain an inexact and speculative procedure in the first instance, beyond the identification of obviously serious difficulties in the children and obviously clear limitations in the adopters.

This points to the importance of seeing matching as part of an *ongoing* process of assessment and specialist support through which emergent problems can be identified quickly and long-term difficulties handled as well as is possible. This points to the importance of the willingness of adopters to work with the agency on a continuing basis and the capacity of the agency to offer responsive and expert advice and assistance.

8 Assessment and research 2: prospective adopters

Much more has been written on the assessment of potential adopters than on the assessment of children's needs. The information about prospective adopters required by panels in order for them to make a decision on their suitability to adopt is set out in the Adoption Agencies Regulations 2005.[23]

The assessment of potential adopters is usually undertaken by an experienced worker, often from the family placement team, but sometimes by a qualified freelance professional.

This formal assessment is preceded by preparation and training, which usually includes some element of teaching on child development. In practice, this phase of the adoption process also provides information for the assessment, for example, training may include arrangements for practical experience, such as spending time in a nursery or school. Information about how potential adopters responded to parts of the preparation and training, or how they got on in any experiential learning situations, is likely to feed into the assessment. The results of the assessment are presented to the panel through the Prospective Adopter's Report (PAR). The prospective adopters must be given the report and allowed to comment on it. They must also be invited to a meeting of the panel before it makes a recommendation.

In a typical authority, the assessment process may go along these lines: Applicants are sent an information pack and invited to attend an information session, which may include the use of profiles of children as a basis for information and discussion. If they decide to take it further they fill in an application form. The social workers then

---

23 Amendments were made to the Adoption Agencies Regulations in 2011. These do not affect the assessment process (Adoption Agencies and Independent Review of Determinations (Amendment) Regulations 2011).

visit referees nominated by the applicants and visit the applicants on a number of occasions for extended discussions. Each applicant will be seen on his or her own at least once, and the social worker will also meet and talk to others in the family. The purpose is to give good coverage to the information required for the PAR. Panels are concerned about the level and quality of the analysis of the potential adopters' strengths and limitations and whether their personal issues are appropriately dealt with. The applicants' expectations about child development, both generally and with respect to a particular child, are likely to be closely scrutinised.

The Adoption Agencies Regulations specify the key characteristics of the adopters that panels are required to take into account. These requirements are comprehensively covered in the Prospective Adopter's Report (PAR) (formerly the BAAF Form F).

The Prospective Adopter's Report (PAR)

The information collected in the PAR includes, in order: basic demographic and family information (Section A); an evaluation and recommendation of the suitability of the applicants (Section B); a series of other reports (Section C), which include a family tree, ecomaps, a chronology, details of the preparation of the applicants, the home study, the medical adviser's report, and summaries of information from nominated referees, other people in the household and the applicants' comments on the report. Section D covers statutory checks; and Section E, adoption competences and intercountry adoption. As with the CPR, the form is accompanied by guidance notes, including those on coding ethnicity. All the sections are necessarily part of a good assessment, but that on competences (E1) is especially relevant to matching and is dealt with in this chapter.

Section E1 presents information on the prospective adopter's capacity to:

1. *Care for children* in order to promote healthy emotional, physical and sexual development into adulthood; to accept the child as he or she is; to provide appropriate care; know enough about child

development to listen to and communicate with children according to their emotional age; and have an ability to set boundaries.

2. *Provide a safe and caring environment.*

3. *Work as part of a team* with individuals and organisations; communicate effectively; keep information confidential; understand discrimination and racism; promote an anti-racist and anti-discriminatory approach to parenting.

4. *See adoption as a life-long process,* including an ability to: understand and meet the child's needs in relation to birth family and history; seek appropriate support; and understand and promote a young person's development towards adult status.

5. *Attend to their own development,* including: understand how their own experiences have affected them; understand the impact of adoption upon them; show an ability to develop appropriate personal support networks; have an ability to use training opportunities; and have an ability to sustain positive relationships.

How all of these competences are covered, and what is included in the assessment, is down to the skill of the assessor. She or he may ask for reports from elsewhere to help with this. Statements about parenting competences should be evidenced and the PAR has tick-boxes to record whether the assessment is based on evidence and what action is planned to deal with any problems. Panels have the right to ask for more information. The prospective adopters must be given the report and allowed to comment on it. They must also be invited to a meeting of the panel before it makes a recommendation.

The relationship of the PAR and the Assessment Framework to the assessment process is discussed in the introduction to the guidance notes which accompany the PAR. It is pointed out there that the usefulness of the assessment triangle is most apparent when social workers are working with families or in situations when all sides of the triangle can be assessed; that is, with children in need and looked after children. This, of course, is not the case when assessing prospective adopters. In addition, the framework does not deal well with the diversity of the prospective adopters, for example, the structure of their family or their sexuality. In this case, understanding their family history and experiences, the relationship of these to their wish to adopt, and their motives in their "journey to adoption" are seen as more important.

Preparing and assessing prospective adopters

The PAR is designed to be consistent with official practice guidance on preparation and assessment, which is summarised in *Preparing and Assessing Prospective Adopters* (Department for Education and Skills, 2006). The advice highlights the prospective adopters' psychological characteristics and the parenting capacities that are of importance in adoption. These include the:

- ability to make and sustain close relationships;
- capacity for emotional openness;
- capacity for reflectiveness or "psychological mindedness";
- successful resolution of earlier losses or traumatic experiences;
- the quality, stability and permanence of relationships;
- support networks;
- tolerant social attitudes.

Chapter 5 in this document, "Assessing adoptive parenting capacity", follows the PAR's broad categorisation of competences in:

- caring for children;
- providing a safe and caring environment;
- working as part of a team;
- own development;
- adoption as a life-long process.

Preparing and Assessing Prospective Adopters is a clearly written and helpful document. Its new departure was to add the recommendation of the use of standardised assessment tools and measures as a valuable adjunct to the assessment process, for example, the HOME Inventory and the Family Pack of Questionnaires and Scales chosen initially by the Department of Health as part of the Assessment Framework

(Department of Health, 2002b). The Dance *et al* study (2010) shows that this recommendation is not commonly followed, although 14 per cent of agencies expressed interest in or used either the Attachment Style Interview (Bifulco *et al*, 1998; 2002), or the Adult Attachment Interview (George *et al*, 1985). The predictive usefulness of the latter has been shown in research (Steele *et al*, 2003), but the transcription and coding of this instrument is very technical. For this reason, the instrument is unlikely to be of regular use in assessment.

Some US assessment instruments

As might be expected, because of the range of agencies and the funding opportunities, the development of assessment approaches has been much more varied in the US where, in contrast to the UK, there is less resistance to the use of measurement and standardised instruments as part of the assessment process. On the other hand, formal research evaluations of the effectiveness of matching instruments are also in short supply.

The Hennepin County Adoption Project (Gilgun and Keskinen, 2005) revised, developed and tested a series of "tools" specifically designed to facilitate matching: one for children under two, one for all other children and one for caregivers. These tools are a series of checklists of areas of relevance, similar in content to those in the CPR and PAR, but with more specific items. The checklists for the child and the prospective adopter are summarised in "best-case" scenarios. The advantage of this approach, as was intended in the Integrated Children's System, is a comprehensive coverage of areas of importance. However, as with UK approaches, no research on the effectiveness of the instruments has been found.

These tools are seen as one of several tools and techniques to improve the quality of matches, a philosophy also embraced by the AdoptUsKids initiative (Gerstenzang and Freundlich, 2006). This initiative expresses the view that matching is an art and not a science.

Comment on the assessment of parenting capacities

The content of assessments of parenting capacities and advice on how to conduct these is much more developed, at least as far as written advice is concerned, than the assessment of children's needs. Apart from *Preparing and Assessing Prospective Adopters*, there are other good and more detailed resource guides and training materials, for example, BAAF's *Making Good Assessments: A practical resource guide* (Barker *et al*, 1999), recently revised in modular form (Beesley, 2010).

Nevertheless, the quality of assessments depends crucially on the quality of the training, supervision and support of those workers carrying them out. Many are reported as feeling starved of training on assessment. This can lead to the information recorded being long on the factual description of the lives of the potential adopters but short on synthesis and analysis. Any policy push on timescales can also be a problem when trying to complete adequate assessments. Lack of adequate training can also lead to the superficial take-up of new knowledge on child development and developmental outcomes, such as "attachment" and "resilience" (Quinton and Selwyn, 2006).

The advice on the use of standardised measures and assessments (Department for Education and Skills, 2006) also depends for its effectiveness on good training on how to use and interpret these instruments. The mechanical or partial use of these methods is likely to be unhelpful or even counter-productive.

Some comment is also in order on the content of the list of capacities and competences. It is hard to be critical of this list. It covers well the broad features of parenting that predict the success of placements, as set out in Chapter 5. These are repeated here for convenience.

The Donaldson Institute's 2004 review of adoption highlighted: commitment; a flexible and relaxed approach to parenting; realistic expectations; and ability to distance themselves from the child's behaviour; and a willingness to work with the agency and to understand that information about the child is related to success. Sinclair's review of foster care studies has a similar list. The factors were: the offer of security with persistence; the offer of tolerable closeness; sensitivity to feelings, motives for behaviour and to other attachments; the ability to set limits; and a capacity not to reinforce difficult behaviour.

What is more problematic in assessing these competences for prospective adopters is that many conclusions are bound to be guesswork based on a general "feel" about the applicants. This applies to anything from an ability to accept a child as he or she is, to an ability to set boundaries and understand and promote a young person's development towards adult status. Working with such a list may be more effective in cautioning against the approval of applicants with rigid views on child development or with a desire to go it alone, or a belief that love on its own will provide the answer, than it may be for selecting those who can meet specific needs.

Nevertheless, assessments are often clearly effective. For example, Kaniuk and her colleagues (2004) have noted that a high proportion of the adopters in their study had secure attachment profiles on the Adult Attachment Interview. Of course, this does not mean that those who did not have secure profiles should not have been approved, but it does point to the need for the assessment of competences and support needs to be part of a process in which support and advice are an *ongoing* element in "matching". For this reason, the willingness of adopters to continue to work with the agency, as highlighted in the Donaldson review (Evan B. Donaldson Adoption Institute, 2004), is central to successful matching, as are the competence and capacity of the agency to organise and provide specialist and focused advice and support.

9 Comment on research and the matching process

The process of matching "needs" to "capacities"

As this review has made clear so far, it is not possible to be specific about the process of matching, simply because accounts of how information on children's needs and parenting capacities are brought together is lacking, as is information on which issues predominate in the decision on whether a potential match is suitable. Some specific research requirements and suggestions are made in the next chapter. Here, some more general issues in assessment and the process of matching are considered. The first of these is on the method and quality of assessment.

Assessment of *potential adopters* has received much attention in the practice literature and in official guidelines. There is also a substantial body of research that points to the characteristics of adopters that are most likely to bring success. Research and practice experience seem to have come together effectively in the guidelines on assessment, although we do not know at present how this translates into effective practice. In particular, we do not know how variable the quality of assessment is, how well trained and supported assessors are in doing their job, how frequently assessments turn out to be wrong, or how often potential adopters whose assessments raise some concerns are approved because of pressures to make placements. However, there are data that suggest that current methods of assessment usually work well, at least at the level of screening out obviously unsuitable candidates and of identifying those who have the general capacities to provide secure placements for children.

There is much less written on the *assessment of children*. This is true for what we know about the level and consistency of detail on their emotional and behavioural development, on their cognitive and educational levels, and on their attachment histories. It has not been possible to determine the extent to which social work courses contain teaching on child development relevant to matching, or on the translation of current knowledge on this into practice and assessment. Anecdotally, the quality of child assessments is reported as very variable. Certainly, research studies using case notes do not provide evidence that assessments of developmental needs are adequate (Selwyn *et al*, 2006).

Because of this, we do not know how effective the *process* of matching is in tailoring adopters' capacities to children's needs at any level of specificity or, indeed, whether this makes much difference. As has been pointed out (Cousins, 2003), the matching process necessarily works on hope and best-guesses as well as on information, simply because it is hard to know how particular adopters and particular children will get on once they are living together.

New approaches such as "adopter-led" matching are trying, with some success, to bring the otherwise unknowable element of "fit" or "click" (Sinclair, 2005) into play, although well-evaluated accounts of these are also lacking. It is hoped that these approaches will have the effect of increasing the number of good matches and lead to better outcomes. The use of discussions around a particular child as part of the assessment process is a way of trying to bring some reality-testing into the assessment process. The Adoption Register for England and Wales is now facilitating and attending regular exchange days at which approved adopters have the chance to see profiles of children waiting to be adopted. In the year from April 2010 to March 2011, 69 children were matched after being profiled by the Register on such days. As might be expected, exchange days profile children for whom it has been difficult to find families (Adoption Register for England and Wales, 2010).

A further unexplored issue in the matching process is the operation of *explicit or covert hierarchies* in prioritising children's needs. The most obvious of these involve questions of ethnicity and religion where conclusions about the need to match on these characteristics may be given priority over other needs related to psychosocial development. But even within this particular area of assessed need, some aspects of ethnicity, religion or culture may be given more weight than others. For example, the perceived requirement to match children with a Muslim heritage with adopters who reflect that heritage may be seen as more important than matching a child of Catholic parents with Catholic adopters, or of placing a child of Welsh-speaking parents in a Welsh-speaking home.

Other characteristics that once figured large in the process of placement may now carry much less weight, such as matching on cognitive level or on appearance, except where this concerns skin colour.

Adoption support[24]

These issues all point to the importance of the question of adoption support. Over the past few years there have been useful academic discussions on how support is provided and what seems effective (Rushton, 2003b, 2003c; Lucock and Hart, 2005) and since 2003, when the new regulations came into force, a support plan is part of the process of the approval for a placement. This assessment must be carried out when adoption is being considered, when evaluating a match, when a placement is reviewed within the first four weeks, and when an assessment is requested by an adoptive parent, an adoptive child or the child of an adoptive parent.

In the regulations, adoption support is to be seen as part of an authority's wider multi-agency children's services planning, and each authority has to nominate an adoption support services adviser, who is responsible for there being a single point of contact for those affected by adoption. This person has a "three-part proactive brokerage", which includes ensuring that the best support arrangements are in place for each adoption, responding quickly to problems that arise with these arrangements, and maintaining the necessary agreements at a strategic level.

The regulations also require that assessments should build on past

24 Summarised from *Permanence Planning: Notes for practitioners* (Adoption and Permanence Taskforce, 2004).

assessments and use the domains of the Assessment Framework: the child's developmental needs, the parenting capacity of the adopters and consideration of the family and environmental factors. The local authority should then decide whether and how to provide services, and in what way, but there is no automatic entitlement to support.

The support plan should set out: the objectives, the services to be provided, the timescales, the responsibilities and roles in implementing the plan, the criteria to be used for success and the procedure for review. A copy of the plan should go to all those involved in implementing it and to the recipients of services (or appropriate adult). The placing authority retains the responsibility to maintain the case record, to manage and support contact arrangements agreed prior to the order and to fund adoption support services for three years from the date of placement. The funding of requested services beyond this period transfers to the local authority where the family now lives if they have moved.

There is no research on how well these admirable aims are translated into effective action. Unfortunately, in straitened economic times, the necessary funding for adoption support may not be forthcoming. Even if financial payments are seen as appropriate following an assessment of need, there is no automatic entitlement to funded support. A local authority will only ever be responsible for funding services that it decides to provide. This may be seen as a necessary constraint on over-indulgent spending, or a loophole that allows authorities to limit their support commitments.

Comment on support in relation to matching

For the reasons given throughout this review, support is *essential* to the process of matching, if by "matching" we mean the process through which adoptive parents *come to meet* the needs of adopted children. It seems clear that the assessment of and service response to the needs of adopters and adopted children must necessarily be ongoing, co-operative and modifiable.

Official and practice documents sometimes give the impression that matching is primarily a matter of finding adopters who have the capacities to meet needs. This framing of the issue should be firmly rejected, not just because so much is unknowable at the beginning, but also because adopters have needs as well as capacities. The current document on support can also seem to view support as a matter of organising or "putting in" services but, as with evidence on supporting parents more generally, agencies and services should see themselves and be seen as part of the ecology of parenting (Quinton, 2004). That is, agency capacity is *part* of parenting capacity, not just an input to it. From this point of view a match not only has to be made – that is just the beginning of the story – it also has to be maintained and capacities and skills supported and developed as the adoption progresses.

In drawing up an initial support plan, placement teams are bound to face a number of concerns, the importance of which can only be tested and evaluated in the real-life laboratory of a placement. If the focus is on the event of matching rather than the process, then possible areas of parenting strength or vulnerability may be over-emphasised or "talked away" in order to secure a match. For example, what do you do if the Adult Attachment Interview is used and indicates some pattern that causes concern? How do you decide whether some aspect of a potential adopter's early experiences is something to worry about and how this may relate to specific issues that the child has?

Seeing support as part of matching, and seeing matching not only as a procedure for linking adopters with children but also as a process through which adopters come to meet the children's needs and their own seems a necessary part of the re-conceptualisation of the process.

Of course, this raises big questions about the recruitment of potential adopters, about the training of those providing the information for matching, about the skills of those co-ordinating and providing support, and about resources. Thankfully, this review is not asked to answer these questions.

10 Conclusions and research considerations

As has been repeated *ad nauseam*, matching as currently concept-ualised sets itself very high aims: to identify and assess the "needs" of the children to be placed and to find prospective adopters who can "meet" those needs. The inclusion of matching on ethnicity and cultural heritage is also framed within these terms – that matching on these features increases the likelihood of meeting needs, especially those related to cultural identity. This review has endeavoured to explore the concepts used in discussions on matching and to look at what research is able to add to the matching task. In this final chapter, the conclusions on both of these endeavours are briefly summarised and some suggestions made on research that might be helpful.

The thorny issues of recruitment and supply of adopters are not touched on here, although these are powerful factors in influencing the compromises that are necessarily made between an ideal match and a good enough one.

Matching "parenting capacities" to "children's needs"

The concepts of parenting capacities and children's needs are the background and foreground of all policy and practice documents. Broadly speaking, it is hard to dissent from this, since it now seems to be obvious that this is what should be done when considering the permanent placement of children with "substitute" parents, even though this was not the way things were looked at in the quite recent past.

On the other hand, there is a lack of clarity on what should be included under either of these headings, or rather a lack of specificity on how finely we should try to match. For example, do we think we can identify potential adopters who will "meet" a particular child's cognitive and educational "needs" (provided that we really think we can assess these) or, in practice, are we content with finding potential adopters who seem likely to provide a stimulating environment and be effective advocates for the child in order to get help and services?

At present, however, there is a striking lack of good information on how the assessment of children's needs is carried out and on whether these assessments are adequate and reliable, so it is not possible to analyse further what we mean by "needs" or how we might know that these have been met. At this point, the rhetoric around needs and capacities can become unhelpful when deciding what to do. In many cases we can only specify quite generally what seems wanted and map out how providing this might be addressed. When we talk about "meeting needs", we more often mean "do the best we can to decide what would best help this child".

Many needs reflect what is influential in the developmental environment for all children – warmth, positive regard, boundary setting, social and experiential facilitation, etc – and we hopefully look for adopters who seem likely to be good at this, although we are often making this decision in the absence of actual information, simply because many adopters have never parented. But in addition, we are looking for some special characteristics. Research on placement disruptions makes it clear what these are: commitment to children who are not birth children; a flexible and relaxed approach to parenting; realistic expectations; an ability to distance themselves from the child's behaviour, including tolerance of a lack of closeness; sensitivity to other attachments the child may have; and a willingness to work with the agency.

The importance of the assessment of the need for support for the new family, and the provision of that support as part of the matching process, has been stressed. Indeed, it is necessary to re-conceptualise the idea of matching capacities to needs to take support routinely into account. We need to move from a situation in which we look for a match based on speculative information and then use services to address potential and emerging difficulties, to a process in which adopters and agencies are part of the ecology of parenting, through which we learn about the needs of children *and* adopters through an ongoing dialogue between all those who can help.

Outcomes from matching

Of course, all the effort put into matching – once the obviously unsuitable applicants have been identified – is based on the assumption that this effort makes a difference to outcomes, and that matching capacities to needs is possible and important. In this, it is necessary to decide what we mean by "outcomes" and how we might know if these are affected by the quality and specificity of a match. However, the survey of the research literature above points to a more basic and depressing conclusion:

> There are, as far as we can discover, no prospective data to show that the effort put into matching children's needs to parenting capacities is related to outcomes. We do not mean by this that the evidence shows that it does not work. We simply mean that there are no data at all. This is true for foster care also where the situation has changed little since two major reviews in the 1990s found no studies of relevance to this topic. (Sellick and Thoburn, 1996; Berridge, 1997)

This conclusion is supported by prominent researchers in the United States:

> Matching is a bit of a holy grail in adoption. I've been hearing about it since I was a grad student in the 70s. With weak measurement, small sample sizes, and crude statistical methods, we have not been able to do much . . . (Barth, personal communication)

> I don't know much that's very systematic about matching in adoption, beyond the motto that one should match the parent's strengths to the child's needs. How pretty is that? The stuff I've seen that's a bit more evaluative says that really any child can be adopted (in reaction to the more sensational non-research pieces that say not to adopt those with Reactive Attachment Disorder). What matters is that the adoptive parents have the qualities of patience, flexibility, humor, other interests and

outlets besides the child, etc. Those folks will go the distance. (Marianne Berry, personal communication)

In describing a tool for practitioners to help with matching, Grotevant and colleagues comment:

The tool is a vehicle for collecting standard information used to inform placement decisions. Up to this point, such information has not been collected in a uniform manner, nor has it consistently been available to those making decisions in the adoption process (agency staff, prospective parents, children, courts, foster parents, etc). (Tubbs et al, 2001)

It is, perhaps, not surprising that there are as yet no data detailed enough to test whether matching specific capacities to specific needs is possible since such data would require reliable and valid measures of children's needs and the capacities of adopters to respond to these, as well as outcome measures sensitive enough to reflect changes in the children's functioning.

But data are also lacking on the effectiveness of matching when more general criteria are applied. This is not unexpected either, given the difficulties in consistently implementing systems to collect any systematic and comparable data on needs and capacities (Cleaver and Walker, 2004a) and the resistance to these (White *et al*, 2010).

At present, the conclusion that matching does make a difference to outcomes has had to rely on practice experiences and opinions, although there are as yet no published data even using social workers' overall assessments of the suitability of a match. It therefore seems reasonable to begin by asking whether matching is predictive at this more general level. That is, do social workers' views on the suitability of placements have any predictive power?

It is not possible to begin to answer this question in the absence of prospective longitudinal data, but it might be possible to exploit existing data sets to take a first look at this issue. This is discussed in the final section when some suggestions on research that might inform the matching process are made. First, some more general methodological issues are considered.

Methodological issues

Many of the observations on methodological issues mentioned in this report can be brought together here.

Measurement

Above, a strong case is made for the need for systematic assessment and measurement if we are to understand and research the process and outcomes of matching. The issue of measurement and categorisation provokes strong differences between academics attached to one epistemology or another. Sometimes this is presented as a contest between "positivism" and other epistemologies, with any use of numbers to reflect or categorise human experiences, feelings and understandings of the world seen as a mistaken or deliberate objectification of individual experience by powerful and vested interests. This argument is sometimes extended to become a rejection of statistical procedures and scientific method in the study of human experience.

There is little doubt that objectification and the creation of social "facts" detached from experience occurs, but this is not an inevitable consequence of the heuristic use of categories, numbers or statistics, any more than it is an inevitable consequence of the extraction of "themes" from accounts using qualitative methods. "Themes" are also a form of categorisation. Therefore, advocating measurement does not mean being prescriptive about the ways in which categories might be derived from data. On the other hand, there are advantages to categories and scales if carefully devised and for which the classification criteria are clearly specified, not least the advantage of tracking changes over time. The Assessment Framework provides one good basis for this, providing that it is amenable to change, modification and refinement through effective feedback mechanisms.

Needs and outcomes

Measurement understood in this way is central to understanding the link between needs, interventions and outcomes, but the issue is what ought to be included and how it should be defined. The Assessment Framework includes seven areas: health, education, emotional and behavioural development, identity, family and social relationships, social presentation, and self-care skills. It can be argued that this broad set of dimensions cover all that is important for satisfactory physical and psychosocial development. On the other hand, they do not include all the "needs" that are seen as important when matching is being considered, especially the question of ethnicity and religion, because views on meeting these needs involve questions of rights as well as developmental outcomes, although the latter are often used to justify beliefs (Quinton and Selwyn, 2006).

In the first instance, we may be primarily concerned with whether placements persist or disrupt. This is, indeed, a first requirement, since other positive changes in development are very unlikely if stability cannot be established. However, many placements that continue have persisting difficulties (Rushton and Dance, 2006), but we do not know whether these persisting difficulties have anything to do with matching, or whether matching problems mostly show up in early disruptions. That is, we need to come to some judgement about what a "good" outcome might be and whether it might be better than it is or whether it is as good as we might reasonably expect.

However, conclusions on what might be good outcomes on some dimensions are subject to debate that may be impossible to resolve. For example, does a trans-ethnically placed child who has no apparent psychosocial difficulties but is not attached to important features of his heritage represent a good outcome or not? Further, might we decide to balance one possible outcome – ethnic identity in this case – against another? This is not a question that can entirely be resolved by research.

The place of practitioner judgements and research

The question of the relationship between academic research and practice experience is a perennial one. Practitioners are concerned with individuals and families, and for them the power of individual experiences is often stronger than the averaged effects that research often produces.[25] Further, research classification may seem crude in contrast with the complexity of individual lives. On the other hand, the problem with practice judgements and "wisdom" is knowing whether they really are wise and whether they can be taught.

Nevertheless, the predictive power of practice judgements is an important place to start in examining the efficacy of matching. Straightforward accounts of practice (*not* just of agency policies) together with some simple counts of success *and* failure would be a great help, for example, in understanding the level of specificity at which matches are made and the frequency of success and failure in the short term, and would add to knowledge.

Research designs

It should be clear from earlier discussions that follow-up studies based on reliable assessments and measurement of children's needs and outcomes and parental capacities are necessary to increase our knowledge of matching and its outcomes.

1. There is no easy place for the most powerful research design – randomised control trials – in this process, for obvious ethical and practical reasons, although the design is appropriate, if not without its difficulties, when researching the effectiveness of support (Rushton and Monck, 2010).
2. There is clearly a need for prospective comparative studies of planned long-term foster care versus adoption in which needs and capacities are assessed periodically over the course of the placement.

---

25 This is the familiar contrast between nomothetic (a focus on consistencies across individuals) and ideographic (a focus on unique differences) approaches. In practice, the two approaches are not alternatives. Nomothetic approaches increasingly pay attention to individual differences, whilst ideographic ones nevertheless look for patterns that might apply in other cases.

Some prospective comparisons have recently been made but these do not include planned foster placements, only *de facto* ones (Selwyn *et al*, 2006; Biehal *et al*, 2010). In the present state of knowledge some reasonably simple measurement routinely applied within practice would be informative and would allow comparisons from the point of the placement decision to be more easily made.

3. For many purposes, within-sample prospective studies of the matching of children for whom adoption is the plan would add substantially to our knowledge, since there is bound to be variation in the degree and quality of matching. Such longitudinal designs have been informative on other topics in the past (Quinton and Rutter, 1985). These studies could encompass both representative sample and single case designs (Kazdin, 1982).

Research governance

This brief overview of research issues needs to mention questions around data protection and research governance. It has been strongly argued here that, regardless of data collection methods, adequate representative sampling of matches and attempted matches is necessary if knowledge in this area is to advance. The requirements of research governance and data protection pull against this requirement when their proper concerns are interpreted too rigidly and inflexibly and/or if they become a way for agencies to avoid taking part in research. This is likely to be a continuing concern, especially in fields as sensitive as research on looked after and adopted children (Munro *et al*, 2005; Munro and Ward, 2006). A strong case on this topic had also been argued for qualitative research by Hayes and Devaney (2004).

Some suggested research priorities

This review concludes with some suggestions on research that would add greatly to our knowledge on matching, and could be done now. Because of the complexity and sensitivity of this topic, suggestions are confined to studies that should be helpful and feasible. Here, outlines of research areas and questions are presented, without going into detail on possible designs.

Broad outcome studies

1. Existing datasets from prospective studies of adoption and foster care in which social work judgements on the suitability of a match were recorded might be trawled to see whether these judgements predicted outcome and whether they provided clues to what was taken into account and what was available (for example, in adopters' or foster carers' accounts) but missed.
2. Changes could be studied in the rate of successful placements over successive years in authorities following the introduction of more organised and stringent assessment and matching procedures, compared with authorities that did not introduce these. Those with good procedures might be identified from the survey in the Dance *et al* study (2010). In the first instance, placement breakdowns might be tracked, e.g. those within the first year, although there would need to be sufficient additional data to make sure that changes in the characteristics of adopted children, perhaps due to the new policy, could be taken into account.
3. In the longer term, there is a need for more substantial prospective studies of adoption versus other forms of permanence in which the study of matching forms one element. Within this, prospective studies of the outcome of trans-ethnic placements are also needed, for example, a three-way comparison on identity and coping with racism between children of mixed heritage in the general population, in same-ethnicity placements and in placements that cross ethnicities.
4. There are a number of new approaches to linking, especially "adopter-led" methods, which are becoming increasingly popular and appear to increase success in finding placements. There would be benefit from taking a look at the longer-term outcomes from these approaches and how they feed into the matching process.

Studies of assessment and of the matching process

1. How many social work courses include teaching on child development? In how many of these is this related to training on assessment? Is training in the use of the Assessment Framework a routine part of social work training?
2. How are child assessments conducted in local authorities? What is routinely included and who is routinely consulted? How is this information synthesised and what is the quality of the analysis?
3. How is the list of children's needs compiled and prioritised? In particular, are explicit or implicit hierarchies of need in operation and do these lead to a downplaying of some developmental needs in favour of others?
4. How are assessments of children and potential adopters brought together?
5. How are support needs conceptualised? Do hierarchies affect this?
6. How well is the job of support adviser working? What barriers militate against effective support packages? What limits do budgetary constraints impose? How well does support address the needs of the adopters, including identified vulnerabilities?
7. To what extent is post-placement support working as a co-operative enterprise effectively addressing children's needs?
8. What is the role of compromise? It is inevitable that making matches often involves compromises between what is seen as ideal and what is seen as good-enough. It would be valuable to know how compromises feed into the matching process and whether these make a difference or, at worst, lead to unsatisfactory placements.

Conclusion

Throughout this review, comments have been made on the lack of good information – indeed, of the lack even of good descriptive accounts – of the assessment of children and adopters and of the matching process. Naturally, researchers see a major role for research in helping to learn more about this topic. Nevertheless, "doing matching", to use an old ethnomethodological way of putting things, is formidably difficult, as is research into it. These difficulties may themselves account for the lack of good information. However, not to try to find out more is a serious disservice to children, adopters and birth families.

There is no intention here to leave the impression of blaming social workers, doctors, teachers, lawyers or the courts for the lack of good information on matching, although the defensive circling of professional wagons does have something to do with it. Rather, the only way forward would seem to the author to lie in careful collaboration between researchers and service providers and other professionals, in which research is not seen as a kind of inspection or investigation intended to discover gleefully "what's wrong", but as a way truly to find out how things might be done better.

References

Adoption and Permanence Taskforce (2004) *Permanence Planning: Notes for practitioners*, London: Social Care Institute for Excellence

Adoption Register for England and Wales (2005) *Interim Report on the First Six Months of Operation*, www.adoptionregister.org.uk

Adoption Register for England and Wales (2007) *Adoption Register Annual Report 2007*, Leeds: BAAF

Adoption Register for England and Wales (2010) *Annual Report 2008–2009*, Leeds: BAAF

AFCARS (2002) *Adoption and Foster Care Analysis and Reporting System: Children adopted from public foster care*, Washington DC: US Department of Health and Human Services

Allen N. (1992) *Making Sense of the Children Act* (2nd edition), Harlow: Longman

Altstein H. and Simon R. (eds) (1991) *Intercountry Adoption: A multinational perspective*, New York, NY: Praeger

Barker S., Byrne S., Morrison M. and Spencer M. (1999) *Making Good Assessments: A practical resource guide*, London: BAAF

Barn R. (1999) 'White mothers, mixed parentage children and child welfare', *British Journal of Social Work*, 29, pp 269–284

Barth R. (2000) 'What works in permanency planning: adoption', in Kluger M., Alexander G. and Curtis P. (eds) *What Works in Child Welfare*, Washington, DC: Child Welfare League of America, pp 217–226

Barth R. and Berry M. (1988) *Adoption and Disruption: Rates, risks and responses*, New York, NY: Aldine Publishing Co

Barth R., Berry M., Yoshikami R., Goodfield R. and Carson M. (1988) 'Predicting adoption disruption', *Social Work*, 33, pp 227–233

Barth R., Crea T., John K., Thoburn J. and Quinton D. (2005) 'Beyond attachment theory and therapy: towards sensitive and evidence-based interventions with foster and adoptive families in distress', *Child and Family Social Work*, 10, pp 257–268

Barth R. and Miller J. (2000) 'Building effective post-adoption services: what is the empirical foundation?' *Family Relations*, 49, pp 447–455

Beesley P. (2010) *Making Good Assessments: A practical resource guide*, London: BAAF

Benet M. (1976) *The Character of Adoption*, London: Jonathan Cape

Berridge D. (1997) *Foster Care: A research review*, London: HMSO

Berry M. (1997) 'Adoption disruption', in Avery R. (ed) *Adoption Policy and Special Needs Children*, Westport CT: Auburn House, pp 77–106

Berry M. and Barth R. (1990) 'A study of disrupted adoptive placements of adolescents', *Child Welfare*, 69, pp 209–225

Bhopal R. (2004) 'Glossary of terms relating to ethnicity and race: for reflection and debate', *Journal of Epidemiology and Community Health*, 58, pp 441–445

Biehal N., Ellison S., Baker C. and Sinclair I. (2010) *Belonging and Permanence: Outcomes in long-term foster care and adoption*, London: BAAF

Bifulco A., Little A., Ball B. and Moran P. (1998) *Attachment Style Interview (ASI): Training manual*, London: Royal Holloway College, University of London

Bifulco A., Mahon J., Kwon J-H., Moran P. and Jacobs C. (2002) 'Attachment style measurement – a clinical and epidemiological perspective', *Attachment and Human Development*, 4, pp 180–188

Brooks D. and Barth R. (1999) 'Adult transracial and inracial adoptees: effects of race, gender, adoptive family structure and placement history on adjustment outcomes', *American Journal of Orthopsychiatry*, 69, pp 87–99

Brown G. (1983) 'Accounts, meaning and causality', in Gilbert G and Abell P (eds) *Accounts and Action*, Aldershot: Gower, pp 23–36

Caldwell B. and Bradley R. (2001) *HOME Inventory and Administration Manual* (3rd edition), Little Rock, AR: University of Arkansas for Medical Sciences and University of Arkansas at Little Rock

Cederblad M., Hook B., Irhammar M. and Mercke A. (1999) 'Mental health in international adoptees as teenagers and young adults: an epidemiological study', *Journal of Child Psychology & Psychiatry*, 40, pp 1239–1248

Cleaver H. and Walker S. (2004a) *Assessing Children's Needs and Circumstances: The impact of the Assessment Framework*, London: Jessica Kingsley Publishers

Cleaver H. and Walker S. (2004b) 'From policy to practice: the implementation of a new framework for social work assessments of children and families', *Child & Family Social Work*, 9, pp 81–90

Cleaver H., Walker S. and Meadows P. (2004) *The Assessment Framework: A structured approach to assessing children's needs and family capacities*, London: Jessica Kingsley Publishers

Cleaver H., Walker S., Scott S., Rose W., Ward H. and Pithouse A. (2008) *The Integrated Children's System: Enhancing social work and inter-agency practice*, London: Jessica Kingsley Publishers

Cornell S. (1996) 'The variable ties that bind: content and circumstances in ethnic processes', *Ethnic and Racial Studies*, 19, pp 265–289

Costin L, Bell C and Downs S (1991) *Child Welfare Policies*, New York, NY: Longman

Cousins J (2003) 'Are we missing the match? Rethinking adopter assessment and child profiling', *Adoption and Fostering*, 27, pp 7–18

Damon W and Hart D (1988) *Self Understanding in Childhood and Adolescence*, New York, NY: Cambridge University Press

Dance C., Ouwejan D., Beecham J. and Farmer E. (2010) *Linking and Matching: A survey of adoption agency practice in England and Wales*, London: BAAF

Dance C. and Rushton A. (2005) 'Predictors of outcome for unrelated adoptive placements made during middle childhood', *Child & Family Social Work*, 10, pp 269–280

Dance C., Rushton A. and Quinton D. (2002) 'Emotional abuse in early childhood: relationships with progress in subsequent family placement', *Journal of Child Psychology & Psychiatry*, 43, pp 545–562

DeBerry K., Scarr S. and Weinberg R. (1996) 'Family racial socialization and ecological competence: longitudinal assessments of African-American transracial adoptees', *Child Development*, 67, pp 2375–2399

Department for Children, Schools and Families (2008) *Practice Guidance on Assessing the Support Needs of Adoptive Families*, London: DCSF

Department for Education (2011a) *Adoption Guidance: Adoption and Children Act 2002. First Revision February 2011*, London: Department for Education

Department for Education (2011b) *Adoption: National Minimum Standards*, London: Department for Education

Department for Education (2011c) *Breaking Down Barriers to Adoption*, Press notice 22 Feb, London: Department for Education

Department for Education and Skills (2006) *Preparing and Assessing Prospective Adopters: Practice guidance*, London: DfES

Department of Health (2000) *Assessing Children in Need and their Families*, London: Department of Health

Department of Health (2002a) *Integrated Children's System: Working with children in need and their families*, London: Department of Health

Department of Health (2002b) *The Family Assessment: Assessment and decision making regarding children and their families*, Brighton: Pavilion

Department of Health, Department for Education and Skills and Home Office (2000) *Framework for the Assessment of Children in Need and their Families*, London: HMSO

Dupre J. (2008) 'What genes are, and why there are no "genes for race"', in Koenig S., Lee S-J. and Richardson S. (eds) Revisiting Race in a Genomic Age, New Brunswick, NJ: Rutgers University Press, pp 39–55

Edwards A. (2003) 'Human genetic diversity: Leowntin's fallacy', *BioEssays*, 25, pp 798–801

Erich S. and Leung P. (1998) 'Factors contributing to family functioning of adoptive children with special needs: long term outcome analysis', *Children and Youth Services Review*, 20, pp 135–150

Evan B. Donaldson Adoption Institute (2004) *What's Working for Children: A policy study of adoption stability and termination*, New York, NY: Evan B. Donaldson Adoption Institute

Evan B. Donaldson Adoption Institute (2008) *Finding Families for African-American Children: The role of race and law in adoption from foster care*, New York, NY: Evan B. Donaldson Adoption Institute

Evan B. Donaldson Adoption Institute (2009) *Beyond Culture Camp: Promoting healthy identity formation in adoption*, New York, NY: Evan B. Donaldson Adoption Institute

Farmer E., Moyers S. and Lipscombe J. (2004) *Fostering Adolescents*, London: Jessica Kingley Publishers

Feigelman W. (2000) 'Adjustment of transracially and inracially adopted young adults', *Child and Adolescent Social Work Journal*, 17, pp 165–183

Feigelman W. and Silverman A. (1984) 'The long-term effects of transracial adoption', *Social Service Review*, 58, pp 589–602

Fergusson D., Lynskey M. and Horwood L. (1995) 'The adolescent outcomes of adoption: a 16 year longitudinal study', *Journal of Child Psychology and Psychiatry*, 36, pp 597–615

Festinger T. (1986) *Necessary Risk: A study of adoptions and disrupted adoptive placements*, Washington, DC: Child Welfare League of America

Festinger T. (2001) *After Adoption: A study of placement stability and parents' service needs*, New York, NY: New York University Shirley M Ehrenkranz School of Social Work

Festinger T. (2002) 'After adoption: dissolution or permanence?' *Child Welfare*, LXXXI, pp 515–532

Frasch K. and Brooks D. (2003) 'Normative development in transracial adoptive families: an integration of the literature and implications for the construction of a conceptual framework', *Families in Society: The Journal of Contemporary Human Services*, 84, pp 201–212

Freundlich M. and Lieberthal J. (2000) *The Gathering of the First Generation of Adult Korean Adoptees: Adoptees' perceptions of international adoption*, Washington DC: Child Welfare League of America and Evan B. Donaldson Adoption Institute

George C., Kaplan N. and Main M. (1985) *The Adult Attachment Interview* (unpublished manuscript), Berkeley, CA: University of California at Berkeley, Department of Psychology

Gerstenzang S and Freundlich M (2006) *Finding a Fit that will Last a Lifetime: A guide to connecting adoptive families with waiting children*, Baltimore, MD: Adoption Exchange Association

Gilgun J. and Keskinen S. (2005) *The Hennepin County Adoption Project: Final report*, St Paul's, MS: University of Minnesota, Twin Cities, School of Social Work

Goerge R., Howard E., Yu D. and Radomsky S. (1995) *Adoption, Disruption and Displacement in the Child Welfare System 1976–1994*, Chicago, IL: The Chapin Hall Centre for Children

Goodman R. (1999) 'The extended version of the Strengths and Difficulties Questionnaire as a guide to child psychiatric caseness and consequent burden', *Journal of Child Psychology and Psychiatry*, 40, pp 791–801

Grotevant H., Dunbar N., Kohler J. and Esau A. (2000) 'Adoptive identity: how contexts within and beyond the family shape developmental pathways', *Family Relations*, 49, pp 379–387

Groze V. (1986) 'Special-needs adoption', *Children and Youth Services Review*, 8, pp 363–373

Groze V. (1996) *Successful Adoptive Families: A longitudinal study of special needs adoption*, Westport, CT: Praeger

Harman V. and Barn R. (2005) 'Exploring the discourse concerning white mothers of mixed parentage children', in Okitikpi T. (ed) *Working with Children of Mixed Parentage*, Lyme Regis: Russell House Publishing, pp 102–111

Harris P. (ed) (2006) *In Search of Belonging: Reflections by transracially adopted people*, London: BAAF

Haslanger S. (2008) 'A social constructionist analysis of race', in Koenig S., Lee S-J. and Richardson S. (eds) *Revisiting Race in a Genomic Age*, New Brunswick, NJ: Rutgers University Press, pp 56–67

Hayes D. and Devaney J. (2004) 'Acessing social work case files for research purposes: some issues and problems', *Qualitative Social Work*, 3, pp 313–333

HM Government (2010) *The Children Act 1989 Guidance and Regulations Volume 2: Care planning, placement and case review*, Nottingham: DCSF Publications

Hodges J., Steele M., Hillman S. and Henderson K. (2003) 'Mental representations and defences in severely maltreated children', in Emde R., Wolf C. and Oppenheimer D. (eds) *Revealing the Inner Worlds of Young Children: The Macarthur story stem battery*, New York, NY: Oxford University Press, pp 240–267

Hollingsworth L. (1997) 'The effect of transracial adoption on children's racial and ethnic identity and self esteem: a meta-analytic review', *Marriage and Family Review*, 25, pp 99–130

Howard J. and Smith S. (2001) *The Needs of Adopted Youth: A study of Illinois adoption assistance families*, Chicago, IL: Illinois State University Center for Adoption Studies

Howard J. and Smith S. (2003) *After Adoption: The needs of adopted youth*, Washington, DC: Child Welfare League of America

Howe D. (1997) 'Parent-reported problems in 211 adopted children: some risk and protective factors', *Journal of Child Psychology and Psychiatry*, 38, pp 401–411

Howe D. (2005) *Child Abuse and Neglect: Attachment, development and intervention*, London: Palgrave Macmillan

Ifekwunigwe J. (ed) (2004) *Mixed Race Studies*, London: Routledge

Juffer F. (2006) 'Children's awareness of adoption and their problem behaviour in families of seven-year-old internationally adopted children', *Adoption Quarterly*, 9, pp 1–22

Juffer F., Bakermans-Kranenburg M. and van IJzendoorn M. (2005) 'The importance of parenting in the development of disorganized attachment: evidence from a preventive intervention study in adoptive families', *Journal of Child Psychology & Psychiatry*, 46, pp 263–274

Juffer F. and van IJzendoorn M. (2007) 'Adoptees do not lack self-esteem: a meta-analysis of studies on self-esteem of transracial, international and domestic adoptees', *Psychological Bulletin*, 133, pp 1067–1083

Kadushin A. and Martin J. (1988) *Adopting Older Children*, New York, NY: Macmillan

Kadushin A. and Seidl F. (1971) 'Adoption failure: a social work post-mortem', *Social Work*, 16, pp 32–38

Kagan R. and Reid W. (1986) 'Critical factors in the adoption of emotionally disturbed youths', *Child Welfare*, 65, pp 62–82

Kaniuk J., Steele M. and Hodges J. (2004) 'Report on a longitudinal research project, exploring the development of attachments between older, hard-to-place children and their adopters over the first two years of placement', *Adoption & Fostering*, 28, pp 61–67

Katz I. and Treacher A. (2005) 'The social and psychological development of mixed parentage children', in Okitikpi T. (ed) Working with Children of Mixed Parentage, Lyme Regis: Russell House Publishing, pp 45–60

Kazdin A. (1982) *Single Case Research Designs: Methods for clinical and applied settings*, New York, NY: Oxford University Press

Kirk H. (1964) *Shared Fate: A theory of adoption and mental health*, New York, NY: The Free Press

Koenig S., Lee S. and Richardson S. (eds) (2008) *Revising Race in a Genomic Age*, New Brunswick, NJ: Rutgers University Press

Lee R. (2003) 'The transracial adoption paradox: history, research and ounseling implication of cultural socialization', *The Counseling Psychologist*, 31, pp 711–744

Lewontin R. (1972) 'The apportionment of human diversity', *Evolutionary Biology*, 6, pp 391–398

Long J. and Kittles R. (2003) 'Human genetic diversity and the nonexistence of biological races', *Human Biology*, 75, pp 449–471

Lucock B. and Hart A. (2005) 'Adoptive family life and adoption support: policy ambivalence and the development of effective services', *Child & Family Social Work*, 10, pp 125–134

Maalouf A. (2003) *In the Name of Identity: Violence and the need to belong*, London: Penguin Books

Marks J. (2008) 'Race: past, present and future', in Koenig S., Lee S-J. and Richardson S. (eds) *Revisiting Race in a Genomic Age*, New Brunswick, NJ: Rutgers University Press, pp 21–37

Massiah H. (ed) (2005) *Looking After our Own: The stories of black and Asian adopters*, London: BAAF

Maughan B. and Pickles A. (1990) 'Adopted and illegitimate children growing up', in Robins L. and Rutter M. (eds) *Straight and Devious Pathways from Childhood to Adulthood*, Cambridge: Cambridge University Press, pp 36–61

McKenzie J. (1993) 'Adoption of children with special needs', *The Future of Children*, 3, pp 62–76

McRoy R. (1999) *Special Needs Adoptions: Practice issues*, New York, NY: Garland Publishing Inc

McRoy R., Zurcher L., Lauderdale M. and Anderson R. (1984) 'The identity of transracial adoptees', *Social Casework*, 65, pp 34–39

Meltzer H., Gatward R., Goodman R. and Ford T. (2000) *Mental Health of Children and Adolescents in Great Britain*, London: The Stationery Office

Meltzer H., Gatward R., Goodman R. and Ford T. (2003) *The Mental Health Needs of Looked After Children*, London: The Stationery Office

Modood T., Berthoud R., Lakey J., Nazroo J., Smith P., Virdee S. and Beishon S. (1997) *The Fourth National Survey of Ethnic Minorities: Ethnic minorities in Britain – diversity and disadvantage*, London: Policy Studies Institute

Munro E. (2010) *The Munro Review of Child Protection: Part One: A systems analysis*, London: Department for Education

Munro E. (2011) *The Munro Review of Child Protection: Interim Report: The child's journey*, London: Department for Education

Munro E., Holmes L. and Ward H. (2005) 'Researching vulnerable groups: ethical issues and effective conduct of research in local authorities', *British Journal of Social Work*, 35, pp 1023–1038

Munro E. and Ward H. (2006) *The Impact of the Implementation of the Research Governance Framework on the Conduct of Social Care Research*, A working paper to the Department for Education and Skills, Loughborough: Loughborough Centre for Child and Family Research, Loughborough University

Nalavany B., Ryan S., Howard J. and Smith S. (2008) 'Pre-adoptive child sexual abuse as a predictor of moves in care, adoption disruptions, and inconsistent adoptive parent commitment', *Child Abuse & Neglect*, 32, pp 1084–1088

Nelson K. (1985) *On the Frontiers of Adoption: A study of special needs adoptive families*, Washington DC: Child Welfare League of America

O'Connor T. and Zeanah C. (2003) 'Attachment disorders: assessment strategies and treatment approaches', *Attachment & Human Development*, 5, pp 223–244

Owusu-Bempah K. (2005) 'Mulatto, marginal man, half-caste, mixed race: the one drop rule in professional practice', in Okitikpi T. (ed) *Working with Children of Mixed Parentage*, Lyme Regis: Russell House Publishing, pp 27–44

Owusu-Bempah K. (2006) 'Socio-genealogical connectedness: knowledge and identity', in Aldgate J., Jones D., Rose W. and Jeffrey C. (eds) *The Developing World of the Child*, London: Jessica Kingsley Publishers, pp 112–121

Palacios J., Sanchez-Sandoval Y. and Leon E. (2005) 'Intercountry adoption disruption in Spain', *Adoption Quarterly*, 9, pp 35–55

Partridge S., Hornby H. and McDonald T. (1986) *Learning from Adoption Disruption: Insights for practice*, Portland, ME: University of Southern Maine Center for Research and Advanced Study

Patel T., Williams C. and Marsh P. (2004) 'Identity, race, religion and adoption: the public and legal view', *Adoption & Fostering*, 28, pp 8–15

Performance and Innovation Unit (2000) *The Prime Minister's Review of Adoption*, London: The Cabinet Office

Pinderhughes E. (1996) 'Towards understanding family readjustment following older child adoptions: the interplay between theory generation and empirical research', *Children and Youth Services Review*, 18, pp 115–138

Quinton D. (1994) 'Cultural and commmunity influences', in Rutter M. and Hay D. (eds) *Development through Life: A handbook for clinicians*, Oxford: Blackwell Scientific Publications, pp 159–184

Quinton D. (2004) *Supporting Parents: Messages from research*, London: Jessica Kingsley Publishers

Quinton D. (2006) 'Self-development', in Aldgate J., Jones D., Rose W. and Jeffrey C. (eds) *The Developing World of the Child*, London: Jessica Kingsley Publishers, pp 97–111

Quinton D., Rushton A., Dance C. and Mayes D. (1998) *Joining New Families: A study of adoption and fostering in middle childhood*, Chichester: Wiley

Quinton D. and Rutter M. (1985) 'Family pathology and child psychiatric disorder: a four-year psospective study', in Nicol A. (ed) *Longitudinal Studies in Child Psychology and Psychiatry*, Chichester: John Wiley & Sons Ltd, pp 91–134

Quinton D. and Rutter M. (1988) *Parenting Breakdown: The making and breaking of inter-generational links*, Aldershot: Avebury

Quinton D. and Selwyn J. (2005) 'Adoption in the UK: outcomes, influences and supports', in McAuley C., Pecora P. and Rose W. (eds) *Effective Interventions for Children and Families*, London: Jessica Kingsley Publishers, pp 253–265

Quinton D. and Selwyn J. (2006) 'Adoption: research, policy and practice', *Child and Family Law Quarterly*, 18, pp 459–477

Quinton D. and Selwyn J. (2009) 'Adoption as a solution to intractable parenting problems: evidence from two English studies', *Children and Youth Services Review*, 31, pp 1119–1126

Reilly T. and Platz L. (2003) 'Characteristics and challenges of families who adopt children with special needs: an empirical study', *Children and Youth Services Review*, 25, pp 781–803

Rosenthal J. (1993) 'Outcome of adoption of children with special needs', *The Future of Children*, 3, pp 77–88

Rosenthal J. and Groze V. (1990) 'Special needs adoption: a study of intact families', *Social Services Review*, 64, pp 475–505

Rosenthal J., Schmidt D. and Connor J. (1988) 'Predictors of special needs adoption disruption: an exploratory study', *Children and Youth Services Review*, 10, pp 101–107

Rushton A. (2003a) *Knowledge Review 2: Adoption of Looked After Children: A scoping review of research*, London: Social Care Institute for Excellence

Rushton A. (2003b) 'Local authority and voluntary adoption agencies' arrangements for supporting adoptive families: a survey of UK practice', *Adoption & Fostering*, 27, pp 51–60

Rushton A. (2003c) 'Support for adoptive families: a review of current evidence on problems, needs and effectiveness', *Adoption & Fostering*, 27, pp 41–50

Rushton A. and Dance C. (2004) 'The outcomes of later permanent placements: the adolescent years', *Adoption & Fostering*, 28, pp 49–58

Rushton A. and Dance C. (2006) 'The adoption of children from public care: a prospective study of outcomes in adolescence', *Journal of the American Academy of Child and Adolescent Psychiatry*, 45, pp 877–883

Rushton A., Dance C., Quinton D. and Mayes D. (2001) *Siblings in Late Permanent Placements*, London: BAAF

Rushton A. and Minnis H. (1997) 'Annotation: transracial family placements', *Journal of Child Psychology and Psychiatry*, 38, pp 147–159

Rushton A. and Monck E. (2010) 'A "real-world" evaluation of an adoptive parenting programme: reflections after conducting a randomized trial', *Clinical Child Psychology and Psychiatry*, 15, pp 543–554

Rutter M., Beckett C., Castle J., Kreppner J. Stevens S. and Sonuga-Barke E. (2009a) *Policy and Practice Implications from the English-Romanian Adoption Study*, London: BAAF

Rutter M., Colvert E., Kreppner J., Beckett C., Castle J. and Groothues C. (2007) 'Early adolescent outcomes for institutionally-deprived and non-deprived adoptees: I: disinhibited attachment', *Journal of Child Psychology & Psychiatry*, 48, pp 17–30

Rutter M., Kreppner J. and Sonuga-Barke E. (2009b) 'Emanuel Miller Lecture: attachment insecurity, disinhibited attachment, and attachment disorders: where do research findings leave the concepts?' *Journal of Child Psychology & Psychiatry*, 50, pp 529–543

Schmidt D., Rosenthal J. and Bombeck B. (1988) 'Parents' views of adoption disruption', *Children and Youth Services Review*, 10, pp 119–130

Schofield G. and Beek M. (2006) *Attachment Handbook for Foster Care and Adoption*, London: BAAF

Sellick C. and Thoburn J. (1996) *What Works in Family Placement?* London: Barnado's

Selwyn J., Quinton D., Harris P., Wijedada D., Nawaz S. and Wood M. (2010) *Pathways to Permanence for Black, Asian and Mixed Ethnicity Children*, London: BAAF

Selwyn J., Sturgess W., Quinton D. and Baxter C. (2006) *Costs and Outcomes of Non-Infant Adoptions*, London: BAAF

Shireman J., Johnson P. and Watson K. (1987) 'Transracial adoption and the development of black identity at age eight', *Child Welfare*, 66, pp 45–55

Silverman A. (1993) 'Outcomes of transracial adoption', *The Future of Children*, 3, pp 104–118

Simmel C., Barth R. and Brooks D. (2007) 'Adopted foster youths' psychosocial functioning: a longitudinal perspective', *Child and Family Social Work*, 12, pp 336–348

Sinclair I. (2005) *Fostering Now: Messages from research*, London: Jessica Kingsley Publishers

Sinclair I., Baker C., Wilson K. and Gibbs I. (2005a) *Foster Children: Where they go and how they get on*, London: Jessica Kingsley Publishers

Sinclair I., Gibbs I. and Wilson K. (2004) *Foster Carers: Why they stay and why they leave*, London: Jessica Kingsley Publishers

Sinclair I., Gibbs I. and Wilson K. (2005b) *Foster Placements: Why they succeed and why they fail*, London: Jessica Kingsley Publishers

Smith S. and Howard J. (1991) 'A comparative study of successful and disrupted adoptions', *Social Services Review*, 65, pp 248–265

Smith S. and Howard J. (1994) 'The impact of previous sexual abuse on children's adjustment in adoptive placement', *Social Work*, 39, pp 491–501

Sokoloff B. (1993) 'Antecedents of American adoption', in Behrman R. (ed) *The Future of Children: Adoption*, Los Altos, CA: David and Lucile Packard Foundation, pp 17–25

Stams G., Juffer F. and IJzendoorn M. (2002) 'Maternal sensitivity, infant attachment and temperament in early childhood predict adjustment in middle childhood: the case of adopted children and their biologically unrelated parents', *Developmental Psychology*, 38, pp 860–821

Steele M., Hodges J., Kaniuk J., Hillman S. and Henderson K. (2003) 'Attachment representations and adoption: associations between maternal states of mind and emotion narratives in previously maltreated children', *Journal of Child Psychotherapy*, 29, pp 187–205

Steele M., Kaniuk J., Hodges J., Haworth C. and Huss S. (1999) 'The use of the Adult Attachment Interview: implications for assessment in adoption and foster care', in BAAF (ed) *Assessment, Preparation and Support: Implications from Research*, London: BAAF, pp 30–37

Stolley K. (1993) 'Statistics on adoption in the United States', in Behrman R. (ed) *The Future of Children: Adoption*, Los Altos, CA: David and Lucile Packard Foundation, pp 26–42

Sudbery J., Hicks S., Thompson S., McLaughlin H., Bramley C. and Wilson K. (2005) *A Bibliography of Family Placement Literature*, London: BAAF

Terling-Watt T. (2001) 'Permanency in kinship care: an exploration of disruption rates and factors associated with placement disruption', *Children and Youth Services Review*, 23, pp 111–126

Thoburn J., Norford L. and Rashid S. (2000) *Permanent Family Placement for Children of Minority Ethnic Origin*, London: Jessica Kingsley Publishers

Tizard B. and Phoenix A. (2002) *Black, White or Mixed Race: Race and racism in the lives of young people of mixed parentage*, London: Routledge

Triseliotis J. (1995) 'Adoption: evolution or revolution?' *Adoption & Fostering*, 19:2, pp 37–44

Triseliotis J. (2002) 'Long-term foster care or adoption? The evidence examined', *Child and Family Social Work*, 7, pp 23–33

Triseliotis J., Shireman J. and Hundleby M. (1997) *Adoption: Theory, policy and practice*, London: Cassell

Tubbs C., Grotevant H. and Kohler J. (2001) *Predictors of Successful Adoption*, Minneapolis, MN: Report to the Hennepin County Department of Children and Family Services

University of Oregon:The Adoption History Project, available at: http://uoregon.edu/~adoption/topics/orphan.html

US Government Accountability Office (2007) *African American Children in Foster Care: Additional HHS assistance needed to help reduce the proportion in care*, GAO-07-816, available at: www.gao.gov/new.items/d07816.pdf

van IJzendoorn M. (2006) 'The Emanuel Miller Lecture 2006: adoption as intervention. Meta-analytic evidence for massive catch-up and plasticity in physical, socio-emotional, and cognitive development', *Journal of Child Psychology & Psychiatry*, 47, pp 1228–1245

Vroegh K. (1991) *Transracial Adoption: How it is 17 years later*, Chicago, IL: Chicago Child Care Society

Ward H. (ed) (1995) *Looking After Children: Research into practice*, London: HMSO

Ward M. (1997) 'Family paradigms and older-child adoption: a proposal for matching parents' strengths to children's needs', *Family Relations*, 46, pp 257–262

Warren S., Oppenheim D. and Emde R. (1996) 'Can emotions and themes in children's play predict behavior problems?' *Journal of the American Academy of Child and Adolescent Psychiatry*, 35, pp 1311–1337

Weinberg R., Waldman I., van Dulmen M. and Scarr S. (2005) 'The Minnesota Transracial Adoption Study', *Adoption Quarterly*, 8, pp 27–44

White S., Wastell D., Briadhurst K. and Hall C. (2010) 'When policy o'erleaps itself: the "tragic tale" of the Integrated Children's System', *Critical Social Policy*, 30, pp 405–429

Witherspoon D., Wooding S. and Rogers A. (2007) 'Genetic similarities within and between human populations', *Genetics*, 176, pp 351–359

Witmer R. (1963) 'The purpose of American adoption laws', in Witmer H., Herzog E., Weinstein E. and Sullivan M. (eds) *Independent Adoptions: A follow-up study*, New York, NY: Russell Foundation, pp. 19–43

Yoon D. (2001) 'Causal modelling predicting psychological adjustment of Korean-born adolescent adoptees', *Journal of Human Behaviour in the Social Environment*, 3, pp 65–82

Index